Dedication

This book is dedicated to those that went before.

Stuart Greenhill

ECHOES FROM THE LAND

AUSTIN MACAULEY PUBLISHERS

LONDON * CAMBRIDGE * NEW YORK * SHARJAH

Copyright © Stuart Greenhill 2025

The right of Stuart Greenhill to be identified as author of this work has been asserted by the author in accordance with sections 77 and 78 of the Copyright, Designs and Patents Act 1988.

All rights reserved. No part of this publication may be reproduced, stored in a retrieval system, or transmitted in any form or by any means, electronic, mechanical, photocopying, recording, or otherwise, without the prior permission of the publishers.

Any person who commits any unauthorised act in relation to this publication may be liable to criminal prosecution and civil claims for damages.

The story, experiences, and words are the author's alone.

A CIP catalogue record for this title is available from the British Library.

ISBN 9781035886340 (Paperback)
ISBN 9781035886357 (ePub e-book)

www.austinmacauley.com

First Published 2025
Austin Macauley Publishers Ltd®
1 Canada Square
Canary Wharf
London
E14 5AA

Table of Contents

Introduction	9
About the Poetry	14
In the End	15
About the Poem	16
Stanley McGaw. County Down, Ireland	18
Stanley	19
The Wall	21
About the Poem	22
Weaver Street	23
About the Poem	25
Murray McCarty. County Clare, Ireland	26
Rodin's Hills	27
Hanging on a Wire	29
About the Poem	30
A Tale Told	31
Douglas Pegg. Tickhill, South Yorkshire	33
Doug	34
About the Poem	35
A Tale Told	40
Ray Gower . Hollingborne, Kent, England	41

Swag	44
A Tale Told	46
Old Man	50
About the Poem	51
John Sextus. Luneburg, Germany	52
Taranaki Weka[19]	57
About the Poem	59
Duncan Menzie Loch. Rannoch, Scotland	60
A Tale Told	62
A Tale Told	64
The Shearer	66
About the Poem	69
Dillon Caskey. Poland	70
Dillon	71
About the Poem	72
Helping Pa	74
About the Poem	75
A Tale Told	77
Clive Wheeler. Māori Tainui,[23] Poland	78
A Tale Told	81
Lucky Chooks	84
About the Poem	85
Eric Darrah. County Antrim, Northern Ireland, Wales	86
A Tale Told	88
Andrew Best. Devon, Cornwall Kelso, Scotland	90
Andy	91
About the Poem	92

Tales Told	95
Kevin 'Butch' Downs. Morori[28] – English	98
Just Common Sense	99
About the Poem	100
A Tale Told	102
Kerry Turner. Cygnet, Tasmania, Australia	104
Exotic Dancers	108
About the Poem	109
Colin (Collie) Hancock. Mow Cop, England	110
One + One	111
Colin Wheeler. Tainui,[32] Polish	114
Brett Sangster. Peterhead, Scotland	118
A Tale Told	121
Donald Alexander Spottiswood Hopkirk. Melrose, Roxburghshire, Scotland	124
Peter Bayly. Devon, Cornwell	128
Hass Herbert. Bath, England	132
A Tale Told	133
I, Woke	136
About the Poem	137
Colin MacFarlane. Finnart, Scottish Highland	138
A Tale Told	141
Roger White. Tiverton, Devon	144
Roger to Betty	145
A Tale Told	147
Stuart Greenhill. Aberdeenshire and England	148
On a Beach	150

About the Poem	151
Puppies in Sacks	*156*
Ben	158
Lighting Fires	160
Morrison	164
Great-Uncle Glen	171
About the Poem	173
Monte Casino Archie	175
The longline	177
A Handful of Dust	179
Supplejack	182
After The Funeral	*182*
Sheep Dip	*183*
Disprin Didn't Work	*183*
A Personal Note	184
Notes	186
Bibliography	190
Websites	191
Acknowledgements	193
About the Author	194
Echoes From the Land	195

Introduction

My father drowned in a boating accident at sea; that was a tragedy on numerous levels but the most significant for me was I did not truly know the man. I did not know anything about his childhood or the hopes and dreams he carried as a young man and I realised the dead only live until memory's last word and an unspoken person is unstitched of deed. There's the tragedy. If a child has nothing to pass on about his father, the father dies twice. This book is a snapshot of the importance of a father; what a boy can learn from him and what a father can share.

Echoes is a collection of the thoughts of twenty men echoing their history and the influence of their fathers. It is not a comprehensive biographical account. Some were reluctant to give too much away about their fathers, but often, the less said, the more was revealed. I did not set out to agree or refute Freud, Jung, or any Greek or biblical mythology, or for that matter, any psychologist that expounded Father and Son relationships. That was not the idea of this book. Though I do cite Joseph Campbell, Robert Bly and a couple of other academics to support a point or trigger a thought. It is not a book about looking back and suggesting those days were better or worse, though where statistics are cited, they clearly do. Don't blame the messenger here. I simply interviewed these men about moments in their lives that revealed a little about themselves and a little about their fathers. The statistics just happen to 'clarify a thought'. And it was those statistics that supported the male-only focus. Finally, the book does not explore the detrimental impact of a dominant social bias on a child's development. You know the cliché-culture made up of thin white Christians who are heterosexual, able-bodied and wealthy, and are favoured over other cultures, it just wasn't relevant. [1]

American poet, Robert Bly, noted, 'When a son stands close to his father, it gives him confidence, an awareness and knowledge of what it is to be male.' [2] A Father's role was to teach his son how to do things—light a fire, tie a knot, drive a car, make a bed, wash dishes, show respect, think of others and whatever he thought important in a continually changing social climate he passed on. As roles and responsibilities blur and modern fathers become increasingly absent, this knowledge is less likely to be passed on. [3]

The rate of marriage dropped by over half in New Zealand by 1970 as same sex, civil unions and de facto relationships were legally recognised. There was also a move away from Christian dogma which freed people to unite in less formal ways. These changes paralleled a dramatic shift in the nuclear family, most notably the increased absence of the father.

The strong correlation between a father's 'absence' and the increasing rates of depression, juvenile delinquency and drug abuse in young men is not surprising. Reports of young men turning up for work and wanting to leave after an hour because their feet are sore, they are hungry, they want their cell phones, or they were just bored are common. It is too easy to blame the youth in these instances when the parents should be held more accountable. Latest reports indicate one in twenty births in New Zealand have no registered father and one in six do not have a father living at the same address as the mother. [4] In America, one in four children do not live with a biological or adoptive father [5] The UK is not much better. It is estimated that two million children have no meaningful contact with their fathers. [6] The children who do have a father participating in their early lives are more likely to be emotionally secure and physically confident to explore their boundaries, engage easily with others and have better learning outcomes. [7]

The World Health Organisation estimates one in seven people (fourteen per cent) aged between nine and nineteen experience mental health issues. [8] Depressive disorder is also a major issue in New Zealand adolescents with seventeen per cent of eighteen-year-olds affected. [9] These statistics make a point about the lack of responsibility some men have regarding their offspring and the effect this has on their children's mental health. Times have changed undoubtedly but those core values passed down for centuries from parents to children should not have. They are the foundation of a family and form the fabric of our society.

The nineteen men I interviewed (I am the twentieth) were born between 1930 and 1960. I believe they are a fair representation of the generation that lived in rural New Zealand. Their parents, grandparents or great-grandparents immigrated from Europe around the mid-nineteenth and early twentieth centuries. Their families lived in rural New Zealand when it was covered in bush and roads were mud, when power and refrigeration came late and horse was the most reliable transport. They lived through the Great Depression, [10] knew the horrors of war and they knew great loss and hardship but they also knew the good times and the importance of community. That history influenced the way previous generations approached the world. It strengthened their belief that the qualities and values passed down to them would set their children up to be disciplined, endure hardships, work hard, respect authority and one another and be supportive of family and community.

New Zealand author, John Mulan portrayed the strong silent bloke in his novel Man Alone. Johnson is the archetype for many men that returned from war 'buggered' physically, mentally, or both. They returned having been either imprisoned, bombed, gassed or shot at or endured all those horrors. They had watched mates killed or maimed in mud-filled trenches, on tropical islands, at sea or in the air. On returning, they fought another war against bush-covered land, faceless banks and hardnosed politicians and were made to feel helpless against an uncertain global economy. Many men found this challenging but they continued to role model for their children the best they could. They were not 'absent' fathers despite their injuries. They modelled old school stuff such as looking a man in the eye, giving a firm handshake, working hard, not giving up, completing what you started, respecting everyone equally, winning or being gracious in defeat.

It was no surprise during my interviews that the word 'love' was rarely used. Erich Fromm, a social psychologist and psychoanalyst thought of 'love' not as a 'passive state' or tossed about in empty or overused phrases as it is today. [11] It is nurtured and constant and develops over time from deeds, not words. And the deeds of these fathers are reflected in their sons and the sons spoke about their fathers knowing the most valuable gift they were given was what he had done for them.

Humour played a key part in these men's lives measured in doses of acerbic wit, understatement and short pithy tales filled with hyperbole. Many became myths. Ancient myths are rarely taught in schools these days, but local myths are still recounted in rural communities as oral history. They turn real blokes into characters whose deeds are often inflated for the sake of a good story. The best is about men who are reckless and fearless in the face of overwhelming odds and succeed but there are others telling of tragedy and loss. Carl Jung said, 'Children are educated by what the grown-up is and not by his talk.'

Local heroes are grounded in the 'is. Children relate to them because they come from a 'world' they know. These 'characters' are admired and quietly envied and their stories, the most appropriate ones, are often repeated in front of children to educate and inspire. Interestingly, the most popular reading material at the beginning of the twentieth century were books such as JM Barrie's Peter Pan, Jack London's The Call of the Wild, The Story of King Arthur by Howard Pyle and Anne of Green Gables by LM Montgomery. These strong moral stories were built on fantasy and myth deeply rooted in a recognisable world. During the Second World War, Captain Marvel comic books were the most popular reading material for children. Marvel was the alter ego of Billy Batson who transformed into an adult with superhuman powers. Billy shared his powers with his sister and friends. The Marvel family's strength relied upon them working together like the allies fighting the Nazis and Japanese at the time. These reinforced the idea that good would always win over evil, and strength comes from unity. Local myths have at their core the same positive reinforcement.

Nineteenth-century Europe with its poverty, class and social conflict, overcrowding, wars and lack of opportunities formed the 'is' for the parents that came to New Zealand. The following men had impressive knowledge of why their families had immigrated. The New Zealand Company used these issues to target prospective immigrants, writing on broadsheets and pamphlets that New Zealand was a 'Britain of the South Seas' but without starvation, class wars or overpopulation. Along with a 'benign climate and fertile land,' it all sounded too good to be true and, in most cases, it was.

In search of this 'better life,' colonists endured three to six months at sea in less than comfortable berths, often exposed to fights amongst passengers and outbreaks of smallpox, typhus, measles and dysentery. It took just a matter of days after they arrived for most passengers to realise the effort and sacrifice to get here was just the beginning.

'History is about longing and belonging. It is about the need for permanence and the perception in continuity,' wrote Peter Ackroyd. [12] Continuity refers to history in a global context but also the continuity of the family legacy. This might include livestock, property or investments but more importantly family ancestry and name.

What's in a name wrote Shakespeare; well, plenty. He suggested the name of a thing does not matter as much as its qualities; however, a good family name still carries considerable value today. The idea of a woman taking on the name of her husband goes back to the fifteenth century when she became her husband's property but the son had always carried the father's surname. And a good reputation linked to a surname from whatever socio-economic class mattered, whether it was Churchill or Windsor, or Smith or Fletcher.

"Reputation, reputation, reputation! O, I have lost my reputation! I have lost the immortal part of myself and what remains is bestial.'

Cassio cried this when he was duped by the villain Iago, in Shakespeare's play Othello. The mirror of the play reflects the regard individuals and societies place upon a name. Each son in this book had a father who wanted him to be a better version of himself and if not, expected him to maintain the values and qualities that upheld the family's good name in the community.

Regardless of where families immigrated from, they all had to build the resilience necessary to endure the hardships of their new homes if they wanted to succeed in New Zealand. Parents impressed upon their children courage, determination, perseverance and a strong work ethic. They learnt to be supportive, reliable and respectful but most importantly responsible. And they cared for their families and wider community because they depended on their collective support and knowledge to face the world. Of course, some didn't, some men deserted their families, some men beat and abused their children and wives and some were alcoholics and gamblers but a large majority weren't. It is this majority that still holds tight to the values of the past and instils them in their children today. Don't expect the merits of these men to be magnified in the text by italics, capitals or underlining, it is not that type of book.

I have used poetry, photographs and paintings to convey my respect and admiration for these men and where they lived. They could have been found anywhere in New Zealand, but they just happened to be living around me. They were wonderful storytellers. There are tales of wartime experiences when a father had so many crickets in his beard he could not sleep at night and a man's admiration for lice because scratching at one saved him from a German sniper's bullet. So, the accuracy of some of the following Tales Told should be taken with a 'grain of salt' but don't overlook the seed of truth at their heart or how it reflects what it is to be human.

We need myths that will identify the individual not (only) with his local group but with the planet.

—Joseph Campbell, The Power of Myth

About the Poetry

This is the first time these poems have been published apart from Hanging on a Wire. They began as scribbled notes after each man had been interviewed. Some convey the character of the men, others the environment and historical context that impacted on them as children. Most poems are followed by a brief summary tying them to the main themes in the text. Where there isn't one, I believe the main idea is simple enough to discern. I have attempted to avoid offending people linked to specific historical events, such as in the poem Weaver Street by using fictitious names. Actual details of those events and people involved can be found in the notes at the back.

The following poem is an example of what I wanted to achieve. If the main theme is still unclear, I hope it will help to define it.

In the End

Red-knuckled words walled da's mouth
skinned by guilt, Guinness and confession.
An aggressive bastard, hard and blunt
as Belfast's terraced houses.
Miserable.
Miserly to a penny.
Drunk at fist-pounding bars dense
with smoke that masked the upright man
'til 'god' became terrestrial.
He immigrated in fifty-two.
Slaughtered and butchered at local freezing works.
We learnt from bruises his expectations
Of women, children and religion, delivered in
cigarette and beer-soaked breaths that tightened
each year as his anger paled to his freckled skin,
to his greying red hair, to tar the inside of his mouth,
coughing stronger than his dwindling legs,
stronger than his arms, skin thin as tobacco leaf.
Anger he chewed to a bitter cud of unfulfilled love,
insatiable hate and gnawing bitterness
'til the squint of his dark eyes stared unblinking like
with horror, him alone in a one-bedroom flat,
realising in the end, none of it meant a god-damn thing,
'cept who you were that yah left behind.

About the Poem

The son's unflattering memory supports the father's realisation that his legacy is what he was in life. It is a horrifying epiphany for a man that is about to die. The boy portrays him as violent, bitter and unloved. The use of 'Belfast' with its negative connotations reminds the reader of Northern Ireland's history of sectarian violence. Describing the terrace houses as 'hard and blunt' draws on those inferences supported by the 'fist-pounding bars' where he drank. These men, fuelled by drink and a legacy of hatred and violence turned 'god' into a reflection of themselves and a justification for their actions. What happened on 'Weaver Street' described in one of the following poems, was a result of that sectarian hatred. The son's awareness of its impact on his father explains what formed the man but there is no suggestion of forgiveness.

* * *

Image Simeon Patience. Looking East

Stanley McGaw
County Down, Ireland

Image: Simeon Patience.

Stanley

He's Irish, 'tis true, eyes be blue
they're a jig and a fiddle and a bodhran.

Humour's a pinch and a tuck
in the dimple of his cheek
and in a lampshade curl-side corner.

He's Irish, 'tis true,
a clump not new
cleft from the old clod long gone.
Respect's a loud silence
so, the old one's left buried
behind a jig, fiddle and bodhran

    Ireland's history of emigration began long before Stanley's parents decided to emigrate. The potato famine of 1845 reduced the population from just over eight million to six and a half million in six years. When Sinn Féin declared independence in 1918, it sparked another dramatic period of migration. The police force took the brunt of the political upheaval. Stanley's father was a policeman at this time. The lack of training to suppress rebellion was reflected in the number of police killed or wounded between 1919 and 1921. Five hundred and thirteen police and one hundred and fifty soldiers were killed with another six hundred and eighty-two wounded. The majority killed were Irish-born and raised. When civilian fatalities were included, it was estimated another two thousand individuals died because of the civil war [13].

    Stanley's father came from Hilltown, a small village in County Down. He described policing 'as a hard violent life.' His grandfather worked with rock and knew about its manipulation. That knowledge was passed on to his son, who passed it down to Stanley. "All the culverts and drains on our farm at Okato [14] were stone," Stanley told me with pride. "If you dug them up, you'd see some very skilled craftsmanship, but I doubt they'd still be there. I learnt and helped, but I never matched my father's skill."

The Wall

The Wall

What a beautiful thing is a wall
dry rock handcrafted to boundary fields.
They say it's a double practical to do such a 'ting,
clear a field, keep things in, keep things out.
They say four hundred thousand miles
of separation keeps things that way,
'tis a cultural determination to be sure.
Gaps of course, a jig of light a fiddle tapping toe,
A Guinness twilight, a snogging show
below silent soldiers standing dead as rock.
Them walls tinkered with something
in Da's head. Said he knew the grain of rock
like he knew the grain of men. That's why we left
the wall in twenty-seven cos he knew
it might stop fists, bullets, bombs,
but not crippling us kid's minds.

About the Poem

'The Wall' uses the four hundred thousand miles of rock walls in Ireland as a symbol for the cultural determination to 'keep things in, keep things out.' Despite this there are 'gaps' where people dance and drink in the twilight, even kiss below soldiers who are described as 'dead as rock.' The obdurate nature of rock and the soldiers in contrast to the joy found in the 'gaps' marks the strong division in the culture.

* * *

In 1927, Stanley's father sailed from Ireland to New Zealand to escape sectarian violence. Like many other men, he left his loved ones behind until he found work and accommodation. Stanley recalls his mother telling him about the shenanigans that went onboard the passenger ship she travelled on later.

'She told me that after they docked in Wellington, the Captain approached her and said she was one of the few honourable young women he had met onboard. Mother was very proud of that.'

Eight years after his father arrived, he was milking eighty cows on his own farm. "I was fourteen when he asked the neighbour what he could do with me. He said, buy a pedigree heifer and get him herd testing. I should have stayed at school but I bought a Friesen. Years later, I won multiple awards for my herd, nine in total. The farm's still in the family. My son Ian and his wife run it now."

* * *

We never got much for Christmas. Lucky to get an apple. I always wanted underpants because the only boy at school who wore them told the rest of us that we'd all be sterile because our testicles were always cold. Later, I was told that wasn't true, it was masturbation that made you sterile. That had all the boys worried.

Weaver Street

Children skipped a rope round and round, up and down.
Catherine and Kate with Rosie and May
stood on the street watching that day
as boys in circles played with marbles
made from Dolphin Bay clay.

Terrance threw smiles at Cushla,
Joe like Prue had lost a shoe
and played all day on bare feet
as mothers with babies washed and pegged,
struggling to make ends meet.

Cheap brick houses lined those streets
made with Dolphin Bay clay.
Ireland was built on those rigid straight lines
like the men who came to Weaver Street that day.

They threw a bomb amongst the girls and boys
still soft as clay, shrapnel and flesh tore the air
swallowing all laughter and play.

Murtie O'Hanlon's leg blew off with his foot and sock and shoe,
he landed all tattered like the others all shattered,
as mothers frantic, dashed manic,
trying to put them together again.

The brick men ran away proud of their day
with their guns, bombs and God
as two hundred and twenty thousand Irish packed up and headed abroad.

Girls Playing Around a Lamp Post, Belfast. Courtesy: Mary Evans

About the Poem

The Weaver Street Bombing in 1922 was described as 'the worst atrocity since Herod slew the innocent'. [15] The brick-hard ignorance of the men who threw the bomb is in stark contrast to the innocence of the children. Describing them as soft as clay prompts the reader to think about God's creation of man stated in Genesis 2:7. When man was first formed there were no 'sides' there was just 'man'. The human element regardless of religious belief is apparent in the scene where children play together and mothers pin washing as they struggle 'to make ends meet'.

The use of staccato to convey the mothers' response to the explosion reinforces their horror and confusion as they rush about attempting to put the children together again. Atrocities such as this reverberate down through generations. Even after the Good Friday Agreement was signed on 10 April 1998, simmering resentment on both sides still remained.

* * *

There are no better examples of parental influence on a child than sectarian and racial hatred. Aristotle considered a baby as 'amoral' and Freud as 'blank slates. Both support the idea that a child is not born bad but is created by his or her environment.

Murray McCarty
County Clare, Ireland

Image: Simeon Patience

Rodin's Hills

Without the able or the means
fettered youth still ghost's intent
beneath a mask of papa and clay
that slips into gullies and sighs
as the rusted chains of time decay.
Phantom muscles still grip his axe,
saw, the drafting gate. Sacrifices
now woked like a battle unfought,
casualties listed beside buttercup,
dock, ragwort, as the hills slip,
gully and warp.
Sieved sand, to silt, to clay the grave
that sings Rodin's pinched form
as the waning hills slip, gully, and mourn
and late dew stars his eyes.

 He sat in an armchair in the lounge listening to a crackling old wireless, Zimmer frame parked in front of his legs. He rocked forward to stand and shake my hand but his legs failed to lift his weight. That gesture told me all I needed to know about his character. A large hand, soft now, engulfed mine, firm with the memory of an axe handle, of fleece, a drafting gate. He was worn and weathered with earth-broken pride. His gentle eyes, more moon than sun, noted me up and down.

 "We're Irish but not religious," he told me, happy to defy a cliché. "Grandfather was a Sheriff. Not a popular occupation being a Sheriff in Ireland, you know. Got out before it blew up into a right mess. Went off hunting for gold in Australia then out to New Zealand after alluvial gold was found in the Coromandel. It became a gold field in 1862."

Murray's father, Charles was born in the Waikato, 1874. In 1898, Charlie and his mate Alf Blake took the rail to Wellington to board a troop ship to the Boer War. Charlie didn't pass the physical as he had 'an umbilical hernia.' The army surgeon operated before he was sent home. His mate Alf was later killed in action.

"Father was a surveyor in the Australian and Thames goldfields," said Murray. "Later he worked for The Māori Land Corporation. Mount McCarty, east of Dannevirke was surveyed and named by him. He married Ivy Jean Corbett and they produced eight children. I was born at Tangarakau."

"Dad was an entrepreneur and farmer," Murray told me with pride. "He built and owned a bakery, butchery and general store at Tangarakau. He made the most of the boom out there while it lasted."

The town was created almost overnight to accommodate workers and equipment needed for the construction of the Stratford-Taumarunui railway. Once completed, the township vanished as quickly as it had appeared. At its peak in 1929, there were around two thousand residents.

"My sister ran the general store. Dad worked at the abattoir, and my oldest brother Ron, worked with Dad two or three days a week. Dad bought Ron a 1929 Ford truck which he used to deliver meat and help move families. Later he set up his own trucking company, transporting timber from the Moki Forest to the railway station."

"When Dad set his mind to something he achieved it. He was a hell of a go-ahead-fella. Very focused, hardworking, and disciplined. He learnt all the skills he needed on the trot. He didn't know anything about animal husbandry and had never shorn a sheep, fenced, butchered, built anything until he needed to. As I said, when he put his mind to something he did it." Murray paused with a tight smile and added, "There was no, can't do it in the McCarty family which held us in good stead for the rest of our lives."

Charles died in 1947 leaving Murray and his brother Doug to run the family farms. Between two of these farms was a block of land owned by McCutchen's. Doug and Murray bought this when it came up for sale at an expensive two pounds and five pence an acre. The brothers stocked it with five hundred woolly weathers. The wool prices tripled overnight in 1954 due to the Korean War which meant the McCarty boys paid off the new farm and all stock in one season. [16]

Hanging on a Wire

Out Tanga[1] deeds chop words
into the ring of life,
battened to fenceposts
like dried bones of old men
hanging in the south-wester.
They're whiskered, bleached grey
pinched to a staple
yet the heartwood's solid and true.

In the window, he waits
remembers stomping hoof, panting heat
yards shimmering, 'til every edge broke
to a whistle, to a voice, to fragmented colour,
to a dash of legs across fleece and rail,
to barking shade of willow and trough.
When he sang banjo with Doug on a goods train,
shunted soot into words of war on his lap.
When he waltzed talcum on a penny round Jenny
sipped dandelion wine from a burlap outback.

Now ninety-three, sunk to his ears
stooped like a bird, clutching a Zimmer frame,
he shuffles down the drive
stopping occasionally to study
the movement of clouds in puddles.

---

[1] Tangarakau

About the Poem

The old man's deeds are 'whiskered' and 'bleached' by the weather of age and hang like battens along a fence. It's a compliment to have your deeds 'chopped into the ring of life'. Fragments of his youth are described as the heat and sounds of penned sheep, his brother Doug singing, the declaration of war and dancing with Jenny. Now he is old, shuffling down the drive occasionally stopping to watch clouds in puddles. The ephemeral nature of cloud and puddle reinforces the brevity of life, yet deeds which are 'solid and true' will live on.

* * *

A contemporary of Murray's, Bruce Herbert, described him as 'the most capable man I ever met. He was an incredibly talented human being. He could turn his hand to anything: built the school, the swimming pool, an airstrip, opened a huge metal pit, wrote and sang songs, nothing he couldn't do. And what he did, he did well.'

A Tale Told

Dad found his missing ewe hooked on in a willow in the middle of the flooded river. He walked a couple of hundred yards upriver, reckoning he'd need that distance to line himself up with the tree as the flood swept him down. He stripped off to his underwear, dived into the cold water and swam into the middle of the torrent. As he passed the willow, he grabbed at the branches and pulled himself against the current to get alongside the ewe. He dug his hands deep into her wool and yanked her free. Both were swept away. It took him a couple of miles to get across to the bank, finally ended up coming out at Rawlinson's. Silly bugger could have drowned...but he did save the ewe.

Icarus Winged the Hills. Mixed media by Stuart Greenhill

Douglas Pegg
Tickhill, South Yorkshire

Image: Jenny Squire

Doug

Legs bowed to the girth of his horse he rides
over manicured paths one hand in his pocket,
the other wrapped with the leash of his dog
called Max.
Morning walks his chronology
when he rode the sun in a chariot
whistled a bark to fill the yards
hunted with bow and rifle
bronced flesh into wild wind and dust.
Max stops, cocks a leg on a sign
'Do not walk on the grass.'
Doug mutters good boy, thinking
about the tapered speed of a chariot
and walks quietly on.

About the Poem

Apollo, the Sun God and God of eternal youth is a fitting analogy for a man that once had a similar dynamism. Unlike Apollo, the speed of Doug's sun chariot has tapered. Once he drew a bow and rode at rodeos, now he walks his dog along manicured paths where a sign reads 'don't walk on the grass'. Muttering about the 'tapered speed of a chariot' reflects his awareness that his life is getting shorter. The setting of the park is more managed and safer than where he lived and worked in his younger days. Praising Max for peeing on the sign is a clear indication of Doug's attitude toward the restrictions that come with age.

* * *

Doug's grandfather, Henry Symington Pegg emigrated from Tickhill to Melbourne Australia in 1879. He set up Pegg, Chapman and Co: Printers and Stationers before marrying his partner's daughter Katharine Annie Chapman in 1885.

Their son Kenneth Chapman Pegg, Doug's father, was the youngest of two boys. He was born in 1892, two years before Katharine moved to Wellington without her husband.

Kenneth spent more time out adventuring than attending school. He had a knack for forging his mother's signature on sick notes until she was called into school one day as the principal was concerned about 'the boy's health.'

At twenty-four, Ken enlisted for the First World War. The Waikato Mounted Rifles had a competition where they raced bareback over an obstacle course shooting from the horse with a 303 rifle. These were heavy rifles. The soldiers had to then dismount and shoot at more targets before remounting and racing back to the start. 'Dad won a medal for first place.'

Before leaving for overseas, the First and Second Battalions had a wrestling match called, 'Cock of the Walk.' Each battalion had a series of competitions to select the best wrestler. That fighter would then fight the winner from the other battalion. Ken Pegg was not a big man. He stood five-foot-ten inches and weighed twelve stone. The winner from the other battalion was six foot and about fifteen stone. Douglas recalls his father telling him that he knew he had to get in quick to win otherwise he mightn't even get overseas.

"One wrestling move that was in his repertoire was the 'flying mare'. This move relied upon his opponent running towards him, which he did, then taking his arm and using his momentum to throw him over his hip, which he did, face-planting him onto the ship's deck. Dad still had the bloke's arm behind his back, he felt he had to make sure his opponent didn't get up again, so he stepped across his back dislocating the shoulder and just to make sure Dad dropped his knees into his ribs breaking a couple.

Dad was wounded in 1917 at Polygon Wood, France. He oversaw salving Mills Bombs. One of the soldiers yelled out, 'GET DOWN!' Dad had been five yards away when he heard the warning and dropped to the ground. After the explosion he got back up thinking it was safe but there was another. It was reported 'a pin on a Mills Number five was rusted and broken, when one bomb was pulled out it allowed the lever of the other to fly off."

Ken was wounded in the head, side and upper right arm. He taught himself to shave with his left hand.

"I remember him swapping hands to shave each side of his face," said Doug. "I'm sure that he did that to impress me. His records show he wasn't a model soldier as he was placed on 'dump fatigue' and docked pay for insubordination."

Sometime after Ken had been discharged, he was asked to front up to a medical panel for them to assess the impact of his injury. When asked how his arm was, he waved it around and told the panel it was great. One of the officers exclaimed, 'This is the first honest soldier we have had here all day. Give him a pension for life!'

Sometime after the war, Ken purchased three thousand acres on the eastern side of the Strathmore Saddle in Taranaki with his brother, Arnold. It was mostly hilling country. The brothers worked hard to clear and fence the farm.

"They attempted to hold onto the land at the beginning of the Depression when wool prices were at eight pence a pound hoping the following year, they would be better but they dropped to three pence. They lost the farm due to the foreclosure of their mortgage. Like many other returned servicemen, the brothers had to walk off."

Marriage wasn't an option for Ken until he had full-time work, a house and some savings. He never thought it was the government's responsibility to provide these things for his family. He was forty years old when he married Jean Sangster in the Methodist Church at Wharehuia in 1933. Ken worked full-time at Newton Kings until he retired in 1958.

Doug spent a great deal of time travelling the 'back blocks' of Taranaki with his father.

"I never saw a written contract for any of the stock that he purchased. He had a notebook where he'd write the details. It was all done on a handshake as far as I could see. Though sometimes it was sealed with a couple of glasses of scotch. There was always the compulsory stop at the pub on the way home where he met up with farmers to talk about farming, politics or sport.

Dad was careful about the amount of alcohol he drank. He'd order a whisky and ginger ale then after a few he'd just order ginger ale and no one would know the difference.

Dad loved reading, he had books of modern poetry as well as the classics like Byron and Wordsworth. It was a passion he inherited from his mother.

Every second Wednesday, they'd have a horse sale in town. When I was eleven years old, my father would pick me up from school and take me to the sale. My job was to ride the horses into the ring. One of the agents would let me onto the back of the ponies or draught horses, most were bareback. If I was not riding, I'd be sitting up in the box watching Dad auctioneer.

Dad would take me to school rugby matches along with as many of the teams that could fit in his Vanguard, which was his pride and joy. Later, when I started competing at rodeos, he would turn up unannounced to cheer me on.

I wasn't that interested at school. When I was fifteen Dad came down to the swimming hole at the river and said I needed to pack because he'd found me a job. The next morning, he and mum put me on the train that was going from Stratford to Taumarunui. I was going be a shepherd. After about five hours the train stopped in the middle of nowhere. The conductor said, "This is your stop boy, off yah get."

I climbed down off the train and found a bloke waiting in a Ford Ute on the side of the road for me. He drove east on a gravel road for another two hours. My new boss met me outside his house in a valley surrounded by steep hills. He shook my hand firmly and showed me where I was to sleep. It was a small wooden bunk house away from the house with an outside long-drop.

"At five-thirty in the morning you're to get the six cows in the yard and milk them. You know how to milk don't you boy?"

I sat in the cold the following morning milking the first cow. I reckon I filled the bucket with more tears than milk. For a couple of months he gave me menial jobs, like cleaning the car, mowing the lawns, feeding the dogs before I got on top of a horse. I grew into that job and came to love it.

We had a large vegetable garden. After a cup of tea and a slice of bread and gravy early in the morning, Dad would garden until breakfast. At the end of the day, it was the reverse; after dinner, he'd spend time in his garden until dark. We were pretty self-sufficient with vegetables, chooks and Mum milked a cow for many years and we killed our own sheep."

One of Ken's first jobs as a stock agent was to visit Mr Robins on Tahora Road and buy his bullocks. It was about eighty-one kilometres from town. Mr Robins said that he would be waiting on the road by the yards at three o'clock in two days' time.

Roads in the 1940s were mud and often blocked with slips. Miss Mary Walsh, for example, had attempted to cross a slip which blocked the road and sank up to her armpits in mud and water. If Mr Timmins had not seen her from the railway line he was inspecting, she might have died of hypothermia.

The best and most reliable transport in the day was horse. Ken rode thirty-one kilometres from Stratford to Strathmore and stayed the night. The following day, he carried on to Whangamomona Hotel which was another thirty-one kilometres. After lunch, he rode to Tahora Road, a further nineteen-point-five kilometres for the meeting with Mr Robins. When he rounded a bend in the road, he saw Mr Robins waiting on his horse by his stockyards. As Ken rode towards him, his client took a fob watch from his pocket and said, "Punctuality, Ken. That's what I like. Punctuality!" It was three o'clock on the dot.

Doug Winning the New Zealand Bareback 1958
Image: Courtesy of Doug Pegg

A Tale Told

Bill Sangster was contracted to carry shingle for the roads, but he ran out of money to pay the blokes who worked for him. So, he decided to enter the local rodeo steer riding competition for the prize money. Watching the early rounds, he noticed one bullock was very good at bouncing anyone off his back. Bill found him in the shoot and marked him with fresh shit off his boot. One of the previous riders saw this and asked Bill what he was doing. Bill told him he wanted to make sure he didn't ride the bullock in the final as he'd definitely lose. The rider said that was a good idea but he wouldn't have had to mark him after he'd been on his back.

Ray Gower
Hollingborne, Kent, England

Image: Simeon Patience

Ray's great-grandfather, John Gower emigrated to New Zealand from Gravesend on 19 November 1839. The ship arrived at Port Nicholson on 30 April 1840. Twenty-one-year-old John was listed as an 'Agricultural Labourer'. He would go on to have six sons and four daughters with Mary Ann Atkinson who he met on the passage over. Mary was a servant and nursemaid. They married on Petone Beach in a missionary's hut. Ray's grandfather was their fifth son and one of his boys was called Gerald.

Gerald was Ray's father. In 1917, Gerald volunteered for the First World War and trained as a marksman (sniper). After being wounded at the second Battle of Bapaume in August 1918, Gerald was given a non-combat role as a stretcher bearer. This was physically challenging and dangerous, involving a series of 'carries', mostly of the living but sometimes without knowing, the dead. Gerald would have had the training to splint limbs, dress wounds, administer morphine as well as address psychological wounds. Improvisation was a key quality of a stretcher bearer, using coats, blankets and wood to carry the injured. If all else failed they carried the soldier on their backs, often through narrow trenches and hip-high mud.

Returning to New Zealand, Gerald bought four hundred acres in 1920 at Kahuratahi at a price of three pounds and ten shillings an acre. "Boom times after the war pushed the prices up before they slumped in 1921–22." Ray said. "The next-door farm was eight hundred acres, all but one hundred were bush. Dad bought that for ten shillings an acre and said that evened it up a bit. It made the farm twelve hundred acres."

The four hundred acres at Kahuratahi were clean but around it returned servicemen had farms 'won' by ballot. A ballot system for allocating land to returned soldiers had been introduced under the Discharged Soldiers Settlement Act 1915. Ten thousand five hundred men were assisted onto land. By 1924, as mortgages increased and meat and wool prices dropped the reality of working on unproductive land hit home for many men forcing them to walk off with nothing.

"Those farms carried scrub and bush and needed a great deal of work and money," Ray told me. "A lot of men went broke. Dad said it was a Victoria Cross for those fellas that came home!"

Gerald joined the Return Servicemen Association to ensure that returned servicemen in the future were not forgotten. That desire to support his brothers in-arms undoubtedly came from his experience as a stretcher bearer. "Dad travelled the country talking to RSAs ensuring things were in place to help returned soldiers. He was the second person to be awarded the Gold Star on the Te Awamutu RSA honours board. Dad served as president from 1947 until 1958."

Swag

Rain thawed frost from his bare thorn ditch.
Tucked inside his beard, wrapped in sacking
he stood beneath his swag hunched
against the bitter southerly.
Somme thundered inside his head.
A piece of battlefield martyred on the road
of forgotten debt.
Bent to his crook staring at the river
at the mob of sheep on the other side
his glazed eyes coloured
to the spirit flaked beneath his coat.
'Cos whisky hears no man's apology
just as a man hears none from rain.

Clearing the land was part of a pioneer's life. Between 1925 and 1937, Gerald cleared four hundred and thirty acres of scrub and bush by hand. His progress was hampered when he shot himself. While out mustering, he stood on a stump to whistle his dogs working in the gully below. He held his rifle between his elbows to free his fingers. As he was about to whistle the rifle dropped onto the stump and discharged. They say he walked back to the house carrying his fingers in his handkerchief and rifle slung over his shoulder.

"God knows how the bullet didn't hit his face," said Ray. "It left three stiff fingers on his left hand which made it practically useless. It was only the thumb and small finger that still worked. The ulnas were shot away in his right arm leaving it in a permanent hook. Dad learnt to feed himself using his left hand, and he could still roll flake-cut tobacco into the perfect cigarette."

"We never thought of him as a cripple. He could write as good as gold and shore a hell of a lot of sheep by holding the sheep in the hook of his buggered right arm and doing the manipulating of the clippers with the thumb and finger of the other. He could still milk and cleared a hell of a lot of bushes after it, but he didn't have a show peeling potatoes, to Mum's displeasure."

"I had remarkable parents. Dad never hit us but we knew when we were in trouble. We had a privileged childhood out here. The six boys all worked together well. You see we didn't need much. Possessions and things weren't important, they don't nourish what's in here" …Ray thumps his chest.

* * *

A Tale Told

The road to the farm was in a terrible state one winter. I remember going down to the gate on me horse to get the mail and saw a hat sitting in the middle of the road. I got off me horse and flicked it up with me crook. Bugger me if there wasn't a head beneath. The fella looked up and said, "I'm stuck!"

I told him, "Grab hold of me crook and I'll pull yah out."

He shook his head and said, "But what about me horse?"

Image: Courtesy of the Gower family. Gerald Gower with Dolly. Tendering hay.

"I was impressed by one old bloke who turned up looking for work," said Ray. He'd have been in his fifties. Older than Dad. Had been shot up badly at

Gallipoli, smashed up arms. Reckoned he was deaf but after a couple of years, he opened up and began talking.

"One day we're walking along the road back home and he grabs me hand and says, feel that. He rubs me finger across the top of his head. Beneath his hair, it was all soft. There was no bone, just skin. A bullet had taken off the top of his head. I said, 'Surprised it never killed yah.' He agreed. Said he was surprised a bullet found his head at all after the sergeant major had kept screaming, 'Keep your feck's heads down,' and I was one for obeying orders like that."

His name was Jameson and he'd taken the opportunity to run away from home when the army called up W Jameson. 'The W was for me brother Walter. It was supposed to be Walter that went to the army, but the army didn't care which W it was, so, me being William went instead.'

Jameson came down from cutting scrub one afternoon with only one boot on and I asked, 'Where's yah other boot, Bill?' He replied he'd cut his toe with the axe. The thing with some of the men that returned from the war was they were so physically buggered that they found it hard to adjust to using tools like spades and axes again. Bill could not hold an axe like he used to and often hit his foot but on this particular occasion he cut his toe. Split it in half. We reckon he worked for an hour or so before he took his boot off and examined the wound. That's when he decided to walk back home. We took one look at it after the bloody sock was peeled away and said he needed to get it fixed up. Me brother Robin drove to the nurse at Whangamomona, but she wasn't there, so decided to head to Stratford, about three hours away. On the way, he met the nurse. She looked into the back seat to find Bill had passed out. There was a pool of blood at his feet. In Stratford, he got fixed up but had to stay in over Christmas. The nurses dressed him up as Santa Claus. Everyone loved this Māori Santa Claus fella and he got on really well with the children.

A day or two later, I went up to where Bill had been working to collect his boot. I could see every footprint he made on the way home pressed into the grass with blood. Reckon he lost a gallon before he even decided to return home.

A few years later, Bill disappeared just like he'd turned up. A loyal, hardworking bloke. Kept his own time, never got behind with his payments on account, looked after his tools, was great with animals, and honest.

Ray was in his mid-sixties when a large punga (Cyathea dealbata) fell on him while he was clearing bush on the farm. 'It got hooked up in vines and wouldn't fall.' Ray placed his chainsaw on the ground and attempted to pull the punga free. It came down at him so quickly he didn't have time to get clear. The punga knocked him to the ground and pinned him beneath. He was lucky the chainsaw was close at hand and still running. Ray managed to get hold of it, lay the blade on the trunk and cut the punga in half. They say that took ages because he couldn't put any weight on the saw. Soon as it halved, the weight lifted off his hips and he was able to crawl free.

He knew something wasn't right when he attempted to stand. 'Pain, Christ, I just couldn't get onto my feet.' Ray crawled down the track to his quadbike and pulled himself up. The pain told him something might be broken. He would find out later that he had completely split his pelvis. 'I knew the only way home was on the bike, so I sat side-saddle. I was about to take off when I saw the chainsaw. I wasn't going to leave that behind. Look after your tools, my father drummed into us.' Ray slid off the seat onto his feet and hobbled back up the track to get it. 'My legs and hip just didn't feel right carrying it back. I was relieved when I dropped it into the front carrier.'

It took an hour for Ray to get back to the house because he opened and shut all the gates. "I didn't want to mix up the sheep otherwise I'd have to draft them all again. When I got home, I was feeling a bit crook and decided to have a bath but then thought, 'Christ if I get in there, I'll never get out again."

Ray's neighbour drove him three and a half hours on narrow roads, winding up and over saddles to get him to the doctor. There would have been pain in his hips and abdomen and possibly legs.

It requires significant force to fracture a pelvis. To collect his chainsaw and make his way home made for a great story, similar in many ways to his father shooting himself. Some say on the way back to the house, Ray spotted deer grazing along the bush line and shot one. He drove over to it, tied bailing twine around its hocks and dragged it back to the house. He credited his quick recovery on its meat.

Ray with his brothers after pig hunting, the 1950s. Image: Simeon Patience.

Old Man

The old man's eyes are still alive
but often somewhere else
looking out through glass
framed youth, ghosting limbs with memories.
See him posed, embarrassed grin pride rolled up
to his sleeves, axe in hand the canopy split
by need and youth's free will.
Another on the mantel.
Summer blazing bronzed brother's pride,
posing with pigs slit to a valley echoing
a dog's bark, an anguished heart.
Days when his Icarus winged the hills
now bandaged thin with grass
melting beneath wind and rain to silt
the flats that ran the river black
with bulls, stampeding down to words
beyond sound inside his flightless mouth.
He is the thing, the thing itself.
Earth clings to his back, bushes his ears cover his hands,
Clods scarred as thin hills slipping like memory
into ghosts behind glass.

About the Poem

'The thing itself' is not something we reach for but something we are. Shakespeare used the line in his play King Lear when the mad king realises that without clothes and perfumes, he is a base animal. Accepting that opened his eyes to understand and accept others.

'To be the thing' is praise indeed because we have immersed ourselves in what we truly are. The old man in the poem is ingrained in nature, it 'clings to his back' and 'bushes his ears' after a life living with the land, wind and rain. In his younger days, he was an Icarus who winged the hills but now, so much older, he is 'flightless' and has only his memories. Nature seems to slowly reclaim him as he sits looking at the photographs.

Virginia Woolf turned the idea of nature's power into the ephemeral. She thought it could take us beyond the concrete world.

'Behind the cotton wool is hidden a pattern…the whole world is a work of art…there is no Shakespeare…no Beethoven…no God; we are the words; we are the music; we are the thing itself.' [17]

The poem has the blunt realism of Lear's honesty and insight coupled with the light touch of Woolf's vision.

John Sextus
Luneburg, Germany

Image: Mark Bellringer

John's great-grandfather, Johann Georg Gottfried Sixtus came to New Zealand in 1843 from Luneburg. He was twelve years old. The reason his family emigrated was the hope of a better life.

For centuries, a salt dome in the western part of Luneburg, known as Kalberg made the town prosperous. That prosperity also relied upon the pickling of herring in Falsterbo, Scania. A dramatic decline in the herring catch in 1560 crippled both Falsterbo's pickling industry and Luneburg's salt trade. Luneburg suffered. Over time, landowners divided their properties into smaller lots for quick money but these were uneconomic which resulted in their new owners falling destitute. Adding to this was a province that was plagued by political and religious unrest [18].

John's great-grandfather took the opportunity to emigrate after reading a leaflet put out by the New Zealand Company. It suggested there was a wonderful new life awaiting with plenty of fertile land available. Free passages were offered. On 14 January 1843, the Barque, St Pauli left Hamburg with the Sixtus family onboard.

Smallpox broke out three weeks into the voyage. Strong winds and rough seas meant the ship took one hundred and twenty-eight days to reach its destination on 14 June. When the families arrived at Moutere Valley, they were met with extremely poor conditions; there was no land available, and electricity wouldn't be connected until 1948.

Johann Georg Gottfried left school at fourteen to become a farmworker. In 1888, at the age of seventeen, he headed north to Taranaki. Johann worked clearing and cultivating bush for Mr Pease. He milked by hand and was the first share milker in Taranaki. In 1921, with the help of Mr Pease, Johann bought his first farm; he was forty-six years old. He set about clearing and cultivating the land using horses and bullocks. John told me, "The best paddock had twenty-six stumps."

During the First World War, Johann overheard a farmer telling his mate at the local sale, 'Don't buy the German bastard's cattle.' This prompted Johann to change the family name to Sextus.

"Colonel Jardine was the youngest Colonel in the New Zealand army and was our neighbour. As a surveyor of some repute, he was asked to survey the line for power from Te Wera out to Tahora. No one else wanted to do it because that section was over hard country. The Colonel was a hardheaded old bugger, so couldn't get anyone to work with him. He asked Dad if I'd help, which I did in the school holidays and weekends. It was good money. He had a V8 army Ute. Going over the corrugations on the Whangamomona Saddle, he'd just touch the accelerator and it would send the vehicle and us into a violent judder. So, the Colonel chucked railways sleepers on the tray to keep the backdown."

John was the Chainman for the sections between Te Wera and Tangarakau which included the Pohukura and Whangamomona Saddles. The Chainman carried a bag of pegs, an axe and a tall white staff. No radios, of course, the colonel would instruct me in his hoity-toity English accent, "Go up that ridge there, lad. Go along the ridge then drop down the third spur!"

Manuka was tall as a house and I'd go along, couldn't see anything, and think this must be it. I'd chop a clearing and put my staff up and hear the Colonel yell, "No, lad…further up. Further up!"

In summer, the bracken would be full of dust, I'd be dying of thirst, dry throat, parched. I'd look for springs. The colonel had no idea of time, suddenly out of nowhere, I'd hear in the most English of accents, Good God! 2 pm, time for lunch, aye boy. What!

Mick Herbert undercut the contract price to cut a chain on either side of the pegs for the lines. The power board assumed 'Mr Herbert' had a crew of men to do the work, but it was just Mick. The poles were pulled up by McCarty's bulldozer. "It was easy going up the hills but you needed a pile of dirt in front of the blade to get back down," John told me.

"My dad had a very English name, Russell Kenneth. He was very like his father, a lovely quiet guy, well respected. It was quite sad back in those days when the eldest boy was expected to come home and work the farm. He got bugger all wages, a pittance. Mum and Dad didn't have a car. They'd walk down to the gate and wait for someone to pick them up or time it so they could catch the cream lorry or the bus in from Whangamomona. There was always someone to bring them back home.

Dad had a hard life in a number of ways. Never got recognised for the work he did when it became an estate after his father died. He got a thirty-nine per cent share milking contract but that didn't pay for the sheep work. Sheep and dairy didn't go well together. While you were calving, you were lambing, when docking you were weaning and shearing. It used to be a hell of a job, so Dad was doing a lot of work for nothing.

He was a great dad. When I was a little fella, he would double me down the road on his bicycle to watch the senior rugby team play. Then he'd go across to the pub and buy me a raspberry and lemonade while he had a beer. He loved dancing but Mum didn't, so she'd play euchre in the supper room while he danced. There'd be dances, farewells and welcome homes at the local hall. I loved dancing too. I was lucky to have two older sisters who took me to them.

When I started work, I made two shillings and ten pence a week. I could go to the pictures and buy an ice cream. At the end of the month, I'd buy a seventy-eight record and bank two pounds. I knew it was important to save.

We never had much, we never wanted much. You never spent it if you didn't have it. Mum made all our clothes and knitted. Now I occasionally volunteer at the Op shop. It is incredible what people don't want."

John Sextus

Cows and Trees. Courtesy of Puke Ariki. PH2006–332

Taranaki Weka[19]

Through the back window, children watch
the unexplained pointing, laughing, giggling
at the handicap of labour shuffling across gravel
to the pub.
Taranaki Weka bent close to the ground grave eyes
knowing holes are not endless. And the sky
is a weight of labour cut with pick and spade carried
on their bowed backs alight with glow-worm stars.
The children watch the pub door close and turn
with a holiday lick of ice cream to travel with unexplained ease
through backcountry tunnels perpetually agape
with asking, who dared to imagine a spark and dug it?
Who dared to tunnel the wind to find an echo?
Who had unyielding violence against the baffling silence of dirt,
rock and clay?
But the children sleep, rocked by a sea of car-sick corners,
past unknown ghosts rusting amongst thick bush,
where initials are left for the posterity of moss.
Over a jug, the old men crane to see
themselves mounted above the pool table,
remembering but seldom remembered.
Taranaki Weka, waiting in hope that their new holes
might be old holes to somewhere else

A Tunnel Near Strathmore. WW Hodge Courtesy of Puke Ariki

About the Poem

Children laugh and giggle at old men shuffling across a gravel carpark to the pub. The men carry a 'handicap of age' from the labour they put into building road tunnels. Their deeds have not been explained to the children who travel with 'unexplained ease' through them. They represent a generation of 'unknowing' because their parents have not explained. This has turned the road workers into 'ghosts' leaving their deeds to rust 'amongst thick bush' where their initials are covered with moss. Like Taranaki Weka, the men will become extinct. A photograph of road workers hangs above the pool table, but they are 'seldom remembered'. A poignant poem about the loss of history and with it an understanding and respect for the people that had made modern life a little easier.

Duncan Menzie
Loch Rannoch, Scotland

Image: Simeon Patience

The Menzie Clan has a long association with Loch Rannoch. Family members not likely to inherit were encouraged to look for opportunities elsewhere. Duncan's grandfather immigrated to New Zealand purchasing two hundred and seven acres at Mangamingi, on Rotakare Road, Taranaki. "He had been an innovative man," said Duncan. "Set up a steam-operated milking plant. Constructed two flying foxes so he could bring firewood for the boiler from the back of the farm.

Dad converted the farm from dairy to sheep and beef in 1953, just when wool prices went through the roof. I bought the farm just before the pound was replaced by the New Zealand dollar in 1967. [20] The value of the land was based upon the store lamb prices the previous year which came in at four-pound four shillings. The following year at the sale they made four dollars, half the previous year's price. So, my stock halved in price and my debt doubled. I had to shear forty thousand sheep a year just to service that debt. I shore wherever I could find sheep. At night I'd come home, shower, have dinner, then go out to the woolshed because my wife would have penned one hundred of our own sheep for me to shear. After that, I'd go to bed.

Three-forty-five the next morning, I'd be up and ready to head off the farm to work." Duncan paused and with a chuckle added, "It sounds hard work, which it was, but you just had to do it, that's how I was brought up.

There is a gully out here called 'Dead Horse Gully'. The name came about when the mail contractor, Eli, lost control of his wagon as it was descending the saddle. They say he had a little too much to drink before his deliveries. The thing you must do coming down the saddle was to put the brakes on the wagon, so the horses still pulled even though it was going downhill. Well, this particular day Eli forgot to put the brakes on, which meant the wagon was chasing the horses which spooked the team of six. They sped up attempting to run away from the wagon. As the wagon increased speed, Eli was thrown onto the side of the road, and when the horses attempted to take a bend, the wagon took them over the cliff, and all were killed."

* * *

A Tale Told

Humphrey returned from World War One without any legs after gangrene infected his shrapnel wounds. The government in the day repatriated returned servicemen back into their communities as quickly as possible. Luckily, Humphrey came from a small supportive farming community and Dad had said he could keep his old job on the farm.

To help him get around, they formed a seat from a disk of timber, drilled two holes in the front and at the back, and rolled it with scrim. Humphrey tied it to his waist and stumps and moved about by rowing backwards or dragging himself forward.

In summer when we weren't doing stock work, Dad would take Humphrey on the bulldozer to clear timber. He'd back up to a hillside, help Humphrey down so he could row around to the back of the bulldozer and collect the chain. Humphrey would sling it over his shoulder, skid across the flats and row up the hill. Once he found a log he hooked the chain around it, clambered up onto the top, tucked his seat under his arm, waved down to Dad, held on tight and rode the log down. He would do this for eight or nine hours a day.

Seeding the hills once they were cleared was a hard, tedious and expensive job. The neighbours had bought and modified a Cessna 180 aeroplane to help with this. They removed the back door, attached a rope to the opposite side of the aircraft, and bolted a length of timber to the floor down the middle of the plane. They had worked out Humphrey was the perfect length to hang out of the aeroplane with the rope knotted around his torso and his stumps propped against the fixed timber for support. As he hung out the aircraft, someone handed him small bags of seed which he split with a knife as they buzzed over the hills.

* * *

"When I was a boy, there were eighty-five landholders from the top of the Mangamingi Saddle to the end of our road. Most of them employed at least one worker. Now there are fifteen farms and three workers. Growing up amongst so many families meant you mixed with a broad range of men. I reckon I was the luckiest kid in the world when Mr Barnard gave me his heading dog. I was eleven or twelve when I was asked to bring nine hundred sheep belonging to five farmers down the road to Hardwick-Smith's sheep sale. Mr Granville, Mr Barnard, Mr Hardwick-Smith, Mr Turner and Dad had a serious amount of trust in me to do that. And I did, on my own, with one dog. What a great opportunity for a young fella.

I was surrounded by people who just didn't know how to give up. A bridge had been washed out and Dad was contracted to construct a new one. He took his TD6 International Bulldozer down to the river. They cut down two huge Beech trees and laid them across the gully above the river then Dad walked the bulldozer across them. I watched him line the bulldozer up on the trunks, tie ropes to the master clutch and put the dozer in low gear. Dad attached ropes to the steering levers and then walked behind the bulldozer as it crossed the bridge directed by the reins.

I count myself lucky to have lived in an era like that. People were practical minded. They needed no manual, they just had to think logically outside the box. Today we're too conscious of workplace safety laws which make us stand back and say that's too hard, or I'm not going to attempt that."

* * *

A Tale Told

Cliff Prescott had immigrated from England and worked with Bill Sprowl clearing the bush. Sprowl lived in a little hut under the road. It was a serious pad for bachelors. Both men worked each day felling bush.

Cliff decided it was regular enough to send word back to his wife in England to come over, which she did. Mrs Prescott sailed to Auckland taking four months, then took a small schooner from Auckland to New Plymouth. From New Plymouth to Eltham, she went by carriage where Eli, the mailman took her out to find Billy Sprowl's hut.

Her horror at seeing the condition of the outside of the hut was nothing to what she found on the inside. It was an absolute pigsty. She claimed it was 'black as the inside of a cow'. So, she stripped off her good clothes and began cleaning. She brushed away cobwebs and spiders, washed away soot from windowsills and off the windows, she polished and scrubbed until the men returned. When Billy stepped into his hut and saw what had happened, he was not happy. "You've totally destroyed our environment," he blustered. "You've taken away all the housekeepers," a reference to the spiders, "and you've removed all the dust and soot that insulated us from the cold. You've taken away the charm of me place. It'll never be the same."

Mrs Prescott was not impressed and huffed indignantly, "I'm telling you now, Billy Sprowl, I will not be staying in a pigsty, so you and my husband can make a choice, right now, the spiders and filth or me!"

* * *

"I'd see these old blokes who had worked out in the bush, they were tough as old nails. Some came back from the war preferring their own company. They had bugger-all possessions and you seriously respected their approach to life. As I said there were great opportunities for young fellas who wanted to work.

Mr Hardwick-Smith offered to pay me one pound for every stray whether I brought out of the bush. This would have been in the early 1950s. One Saturday I brought out thirteen woolly wethers. Working on the farm I was only making six pounds a week, so thirteen pounds was pretty good money for one day's work. I recall one sheep alone carrying twenty-eight pounds of wool. Mr Hardwick-Smith was getting one pound for one pound of wool at the time, so he was making a good profit, but I didn't care.

I think you learn to take risks from watching others, that's the same with challenging yourself and pushing boundaries. At boarding school in Whanganui, my mate and I decided to visit the local freezing works to see if we could get free meat. We turned up impeccably dressed in our school uniforms and we both carried clipboards. You can just about get into anywhere with a clipboard, a white shirt and a school tie. The receptionist said the boss was in a meeting; we would have to wait but it wasn't for long. We shook his hand firmly, looked him in the eye and told him we were researching the meat industry as we were thinking of careers in it. He was most impressed and said he'd show us around." 'If we time it right, boys, you might get lunch.' Lunch in those days was a three-course meal.

We left after lunch with a couple of meat packs each and our ears filled with praise for showing so much initiative. That summer we used the same technique to visit the local racecourse where we were given a VIP tour followed by a member's club lunch.

I've had a great life. It's been a lot of fun. My father along with the other men I knew gave me a foundation to base my life upon that was second to none. That's where my confidence to find the edge of my life and to challenge boundaries came from.

Nietzsche said, 'The big problem of any young person's life is to have models to suggest possibilities.' [21]

The Shearer

Dawn again.
I dress.
Stretch yesterday's day's aching hands,
shoulders, legs, my back.
Gang's already at the shed beer stale
sitting in the smell of bacon.
Magpies dawn the chorus.
Dogs bark the yards full
a count of minutes to fill my day.
I climb the board to the swinging door.
Back bent, knees tight, hand splayed
over hot skin
my neck turns with the blade
every stroke a count
a second a minute
a cent dripping sweat,
to get ahead,
to pay bank debt back.
Click.
The flapping gate clocks one more
blurs the shepherd's holler and whistle
as dogs scratch the air with a bark.
My shoulders burn, wristy hand
swollen to the piece.
Click.
Straining, I drag another
counter ticks my debt away.
Smoko.

Towel wet. Sweet cordial soothes.
We talk in numbers, my age, my pain
'til boss calls, 'shepherds penned my time again.'
I climb the board to the swinging door
and take one more.

The Shearer. Courtesy of Jo Stallard Oil on Board

About the Poem

Each day of shearing is a physical and psychological battle for the shearer. He describes his day with simple thoughts as though even thinking them is exhausting, 'Dawn again. I dress.' He is the last to go down to the shed with a body that strains each time he drags a sheep from a pen to shear. Verbs convey the effort, 'bent', 'climb', 'burn'. These coupled with adjectives such as 'hot' and 'dripping' describe a man who is struggling with his 'age' and 'pain' to pay his debt back to the bank. The lines 'shepherds penned time again' and 'a count of minutes to fill my day' suggests the bank has penned him to time in order to repay his debt. There is a possible undercurrent here that like the sheep he is also being fleeced.

There is enough detail in this poem to give it authenticity; the magpies chorus, smell of bacon, barking dogs and the pain often carried by shearers who are consistently bent and holding a handpiece.

Dillon Caskey
Poland

Image: Simeon Patience

Dillon

Speckled old belly, plump with summer days
hangs beneath a ceiling sky, breaking tree, leaf, cloud
to sup a fly pointe dancing above.
Pricked, he surges between bones of rock
To the mouth of the last sun shattering willows,
knocking silent drumsticks against cicadas
rasping their last verse.
Line cuts Currach, leaf boat drifting
aflame in the setting sun
top lip trophied with battles
as life's current flows past the gasping shallows
where a large heart beats
in the hands of proud boys.

Trout
Courtesy, Jo Stallard. Pencil & Gouache

About the Poem

There are numerous references in the book to lives 'plump with summer days.' Here the trout, like Dillon is plump with them suggesting he has had a happy life. I was told Dillon caught his last trout when he was ninety years old. In the poem the trout, even in the throes of dying still 'surges' and 'shatters' and 'knocks' against life. And it wasn't an easy life suggested by his top lip 'trophied with battles'. A testament to all the battles he fought he won. At his death, 'in the gasping shallows' his 'large heart' is passed on to his 'proud boys.'

Remember the first poem titled In the End? It describes the father's realisation that the terrible legacy of his life is all that will be left after his death. Poems such as 'Dillon' and 'Hanging on a Wire' describe the positive impressions men have left behind. Dillon's heart is still beating his legacy which is now in the hands of his boys just as Murray McCarty's is 'chopped into the ring of life.'

* * *

The original family name was Crofskey. It sounded too German for Phillip Bertram who changed it to Caskey during the First World War. Phillip was born in 1897. His wife, Grace Elizabeth had eleven children, six were boys and one of them was Dillon. Five boys worked together to build their own timber mill.

"Necessity created it!" laughed Dillon. "We used a Chevrolet 4, then a Chevrolet 6. Connected the drive shaft with a band to the blade. Bolted this to that and tied it all down with that. Produced one thousand nine hundred revs in top gear. We used a 44-gallon drum of water for cooling. Worked logger and worked post splitter, worked batten maker. Could make three thousand battens a day, mostly Macrocarpa. We all worked bloody hard. Some orders were huge, like Hosking's took thirty-five thousand fence battens.

Before we set that up, I was paid to clear bush. By twenty I had cleared two hundred acres. I can remember cutting down a Rimu. The first limb was fifty feet up. I counted the growth rings once the tree had fallen. It was six hundred and ten years old." Dillon paused and added on reflection, "We cut it down in ten minutes."

Felling trees in the bush could be dangerous. Tawa was called Mother's Widow. [22] Often after you'd cut the scarf the tree split, and slid down it, splaying branches and foliage across the bush beneath.

"Killed plenty of blokes," Dillon told me. "I remember helping Pa. He was fixed on chopping down a Tawa and had me cutting away supplejack vines with an axe from around it. I was struggling to make headway when Pa yelled out, 'Run!!! Run Dillon!' I heard this massive crack splitting the air and all around me branches and foliage flattened the bush. Miraculously, it missed me."

Helping Pa

Ma warned from the porch, "Not too fast now, Dil."
Pa sat on his Indian Scout me on the back, sidecar choka with tools.
Ma calling, "You hear me, Dil?"
Him saying, "Hold on tight, boy,"
to a caterpillar in a singlet, hairy, hard and cold
or did he mean to the six-foot M2 saw and crowbar balanced across my thighs?
We were off to cut trees down at Atkinson's.
"Be careful, you boys! Dil, you hear me?"
Around corners, Pa deep-throttled him leaning low like we were being chased
or doing the chasing cos, he had that restlessness
like he wanted to get somewhere.
Then me foot slipped; big toe split beneath the nail
blood gushing me crying out.
Ma said, "SLOW! I've lost me bloody toe!"
Pa saying over his shoulder, "It'll be right."
Mrs Atkinson said, "You should go to hospital."
Pa saying, "Nah, he'll be alright."
Mrs Atkinson's sticking plaster got lost in the mud.
Pa saying, "Here, boy, wrap me handkerchief tight; it'll be alright."

About the Poem

It is clear the narrator is young by his simple statements, incorrect grammar such as 'me foot slipped' and the simple description of his father as a 'caterpillar…hairy, hard and cold'. The hyperbole coupled with the expletive 'I've lost my bloody toe' reflects the influence of his father and probably other men around him. The father's casual indifference towards his son's stubbed toe is conveyed by the repetition of 'It'll be alright'. He does care enough to offer his handkerchief. It is important to remember this was at a time when a serious injury was shooting yourself, breaking a pelvis, chopping off a toe or being blown up, and a time when hours worked meant food on the table and debt was repaid.

Imitating Dad. Courtesy of Pegg Family

A Tale Told

"Haymaking on one hill of the farm was tricky as it dropped away to Lake Ratapiko. Pa didn't want bales rolling down into the water because it was a bastard to get them out. He'd get us boys to guard that boundary as the baler circled the hill. We were tough little buggers, always challenging ourselves. After a few years, we stopped following the baler to secure the bales as they dropped out. Instead, we'd line up at the bottom of the hill and wait for bales to roll down. As they did, they'd pick up speed and start bouncing, tumbling, getting faster and faster and you'd line one up ready to tackle it. You were ten or twelve years old watching this weight of dry grass bounding towards you. Mostly you caught them but occasionally, very rarely you were knocked over, left winded and gasping as it continued down towards the lake, everyone watching, calling, Save the bale!"

Dillon's sons Warren and Victor shared a few quick points about their dad. "The good thing about Dad was he knew there were two ways of doing things, his way and the wrong way. Just as there were two opinions, his opinion and the wrong opinion.

Every farm Dad worked on he told us he had left buckets filled with good advice all over them.

He was a great Dad. We shared time with him trout fishing, camping and playing cards. Cards were every Thursday night at his and Mum's. For twenty-five years, we'd try and prove that he wasn't the best at everything. Those evenings were filled with bullshit and laughter. Mum baked fresh during the day and looked forward to those evenings more and more as time passed."

Clive Wheeler
Māori Tainui,[23] Poland

Image: Simeon Patience

Clive and his brother Colin spent most school holidays on their grandfather's farm. "We'd be car-sick all the way out and all the way back home again. Sometimes we'd take the two-hour train trip from Stratford. Grandfather Roguski was the toughest man I ever knew. He had a short…well no, he had no neck, large chunks of muscle made his forearms and shoulders bulge, he would work from daylight to dark…we hardly saw him. He was still hand milking until power arrived in the late 1940s."

William, Clive's father, grew up and lived in Stratford. "We learnt how to work watching him. He would leave early and come home late. He worked in camps for tuppence (roughly twenty cents) an hour during the Depression, mostly on roads. If he saw any branches on the side of the road on the way home, he'd stop and throw them in the truck, bring them back and saw them up for firewood. After tea, he'd be out in the veggie garden until dark. We had a huge garden.

The Depression meant you had to work. If you didn't hold on to your job, it was frowned upon. Everyone in town would know if you lost it. It was a matter of pride. Part of the ethos we were brought up with was to work hard, provide for our family and to face up to our responsibilities. People judged you on that.

Between 1950–53, sheep farmers received one pound for one pound of wool because the Americans were stockpiling it due to the Korean War. [24] Those prices lifted mortgages off most New Zealand sheep farmers. Wool buyers from all over the world would come to New Zealand wool sales. Taranaki's was in the Whanganui Town Hall.

Prompt day' was the day all wool buyers had to pay their accounts. I was working for Newton Kings and remember when one wool sale cheque came in. 'Take this to the bank,' the manager instructed. 'It's the most money you'll ever have in your hand.' I looked at the amount written on the piece of paper, £250,000. I can tell you it was a damned quick trip up Broadway to the bank.

Today that amount equates to over six million dollars. Success on the farm meant money was spent in town. Newton Kings and then Farmers were a vital link in doing that."

Clive spoke with admiration about the farming communities he visited as a stock agent. "They carried an unspoken sense of community. They shared ups and downs; this was a huge part of what made New Zealand producers successful. Nothing came easy for them, which meant everything had value, from buying a pair of work boots, a shearing handpiece, a new dress, shirt, or toy for a child. They had a great respect for their parents and grandparents. The men who went to war were linked by that experience. Each family's loss was the community's and was not forgotten. Going to church for some was not for the Sunday service but to meet up with others in the district. Celebrating achievements, birthdays, weddings and homecomings brought the community to the local hall. As small farms became less economic and were swallowed up by expanding neighbours, rural communities shrank, schools closed, and people moved away."

A Tale Told

WILLIAM P SHINE was a remittance man, so the story went. Kicked out of home in England by his family, he was sent to New Zealand. No one really knew how he ended up farming on Tangarakau Road. He was a tall man, over six foot four and had the demeanour of an educated man with a theatrical inclination. His smile was mesmerising, as it often flashed his gold teeth, which, when he went to town, picked up the gold fob chain attached to his watch in his waistcoat pocket.

William took the train into town once a month. He'd be smartly dressed in a black suit, polished black shoes, bow tie and his black hair oiled and swished back. By the time the late afternoon train departed, Bill had totally undone himself, becoming drunk and dishevelled. He'd sleep it off during the trip home, clamber down onto the rail tracks when the driver stopped opposite his road, then stumble home to a tumbled-down shack.

He farmed large Cheviot Sheep and took advantage of land that belonged to The Department of Lands and Survey, [25] in the Tangarakau Gorge. It was a strip known as the 'long acre'. Clive told me, "When Shine's sheep grazed the long acre, it was clean as a whistle, no weeds or scrub. When he was told to remove his stock, within two years it had returned to manuka, thistle, blackberry, and gorse."

The Stock Act of 1908 required sheep farmers to dip their sheep at a specified time to kill lice, flies and ked. Penalties were issued to farmers if sheep were found to be infected at sales.

William was confronted by a stock agent who insisted he dip his sheep otherwise they would not be transported to the sale.

"Well," Shine began, "you know I was in the war. Early one morning, I was against the trench wall looking out for any Germans. I had my Enfield lined up through my loophole ready to shoot. As I took a deep breath ready to discharge my weapon, I was bit on the side of my neck. The moment I moved to scratch, a bullet pierced the loophole, ripped the air across my ear and hit the clay bank *behind me. That phthirapteran saved my life, boys." With a light frown and sly smile, he added. "And you are asking me to kill them! I don't think so."*

* * *

Clive wasn't a farmer, but he spent most of his working career with them. "They were amazing people," he told me. "Still are. Like my father, they worked hard, they suffered through the Depression and wars like him but endured the best they could. Those generations had a remarkable ability to recall dates, names, and detailed accounts of local, national, and international events." History impacted upon them directly; it was real and practical; it was not an abstraction you saw on a screen.

Old Shed
Image: Simeon Patience

Lucky Chooks

Pop steps onto the porch wearing slippers
thinks they are cowboy boots
but they're not. They're slippers.
Now he sits in his wicker chair watching sparrows and chooks
follow what is natural under trimmed hedges across weedless lawns.
You ask if he wants tea.
'Not in the saddle dear save the crown jewels.'
That's a joke of course but he believes it.
Seriously.
See his soft hands tighten on the reign's
eyes raging bright against his pallid skin
as his stallion charges into the mouth of a smile.
Hollers, "Bloody chooks! Out of me way!"
Hands flapping, "Shoo, shoo!" But not for long.
Ma, all clothes pegs and apron strings turns
From swinging pyjamas, undies, and diapers.
Collared shirts and ties don't live here anymore.
Calls, "Time for a biscuit and tea, aye love?"
Time! That's a baffled silence for Pop.
You watch him finger crumbs on the tablecloth
then he blurts, "Lucky chooks!"

About the Poem

'Lucky Chooks' is the title but also the key to understanding the father. The father's joy comes from riding his make-believe horse across a 'weedless lawn' frightening the chooks which he calls 'lucky'. They are lucky because unlike him they do 'what is natural' under the hedges and across the lawn. The father's dementia is implied by his belief the slippers he wears are cowboy boots, and that he is sitting in a saddle riding a horse. Blurting 'lucky chooks' indicates he is still lucid enough to discern the difference between the unnatural life he had lived and the natural freedom of sparrows and chooks. Like many of the other poems, time is an important theme here. Briefly his eyes rage as his 'stallion charges' in his mind's eye. It reminds us that he could have been a cowboy but instead, he chose a different career, one that demanded he wore collared shirts and ties. Time has passed and the opportunity gone; now he sits handicapped by age, dementia and incontinence.

Eric Darrah
County Antrim, Northern Ireland, Wales

Image: Simeon Patience

The Darrah family moved from Ireland to Liverpool in the early 1800s. Eric's father, Charlie was born in 1891 and raised in Wales by his mother's sister. At the age of eighteen, he sailed from London to New Zealand on the SS Turakina, arriving with a very broad Welsh accent, knee-length corduroy trousers and a carpet bag with few possessions. He was an 'assisted passenger' contracted to later work on a farm.

Charlie had two stints serving in the army during the First World War. In October 1914, he sailed out of Wellington on the SS Arawa for Devonport, England. In Gallipoli, he was seriously injured by gunshot wounds to his right leg, left hand and face. This forced Charlie to return to New Zealand to convalesce. Once he had recovered, he re-enlisted and was sent to fight in Egypt travelling on the Willochra. [26]

Charlie was a rifleman and a 'Batman' for those in command. He was tasked with running sensitive information and instructions between the trenches in France. Being a man of slight stature, he was a fast runner, extremely nimble and a very good horseman.

"Dad wasn't an active man," Eric recalls, "he was gassed during the First World War. For six months a year, during summer, he was confined to an oxygen tent then in winter he was allowed out. So, my summer was winter when dad was out and winter was my summer when he was in the tent. He was a short wiry fella, only five foot, two inches. After the war, he worked at Huinga Dairy factory and later at Pettigrew's Florist selling plants. He was part of a team that established trees and gardens for State Advances, a government department set up in 1903 for the purpose of issuing cheap loans to farmers and settlers."

"Dad looked after the local pool hall when the manager was away. Mr Rod Curry was one of the patrons. He wore a big Stetson hat and high-heeled boots, stood six foot six, and had hands like dinner plates. Father confronted him over something he was doing during a game. Rod wasn't used to being pulled up, especially by some little fella half his size. He confronted Dad. In the silence of the hall, Dad didn't bat an eyelid, he stood his ground and faced him off. I would have been twelve years old at the time and was very impressed that Dad stood up for what was right. Mr Curry finally laughed and conceded to letting it go."

A Tale Told

Archie Marr walked his horse and cart through town with five dogs trotting around him. He was a little Welsh man with a broad accent and language that turned the town air as blue as winter smoke. All his dogs were named after the words they provoked, which made mothers in town stick their fingers over their children's ears whenever he passed.

"As young fellas, we'd been feeling down at the racecourse. We had pulled a trolley of eel's halfway home when it suddenly occurred to us that our mothers weren't interested in cooking them. In fact, they had told us in no uncertain terms they did not want to see the slimy things ever again. So, we all agreed to drop them at the pound's trough instead. It seemed a natural place to leave them. The pound was a fenced block of land on the edge of town, set aside for stock to be kept overnight."

"We had just dropped the eels in when Archie brought his gig into the pound so his horse could have a drink. We watched him clamber off his seat and tie the reins to the wheel to stop it from moving. He had just taken his tobacco out of his pocket when the horse noticed the eels. Well, all hell broke loose. The more we watched, the more distance we made between us and Archie, as his language lit up the neighbourhood. Lights flicked on from house to house as he told the world what he thought of the prank."

"One of the lasting memories I have of Dad is sitting with him under a tree in Evelyn Moon's Garden. She was a music teacher and wouldn't tolerate any noise outside her window when she was teaching. So, Dad stopped work and bought a bottle of Green River Lemonade and we sat in the shade and shared it."

'Just as iron is forged by fire, so too is a man shaped by the trials and tribulations of life.'

'Iron John' by Robert Bly. [1]

Horse and Cart 1890-1910
Courtesy of Puke Ariki Library: PHO0210_0394

Andrew Best
Devon, Cornwall Kelso, Scotland

Image: Simeon Patience

Andy

Knowing death is forever they walked the hill like tailors
stitching post and wire to boundary their lives.
And the wind kicks the hills blunt to free bones that vein
to gullies made lush in the son's green eyes.

Knowing death is forever, Gorgy[1] still tip-toes on whistle,
over grass-tips, shoulder blades wheeling the silent stare
to flock the yards where dogs lap shaded trough into
Woollaston hills cicada paint thick with sound.

Knowing death is forever, horses' ghost the stables empty shoes
where farthing and shilling jingled
to hammer blows in dust men's pockets.

Knowing death is forever he keeps close the frocked sun
that never left his father's eye, no shadow cast nor cloud
ever masked the wink she tempted him by.

Knowing death is endless, long grey ash in the blood-
brown soil veins to the pool where herons feed
on Hamlet's kings, that fly in the sky of his son's eye.

Knowing dead men's seed doesn't grow on battlefields
and a child of dust is a dead man unstitched,
he looks to the ridgeline stapled to the sky,
feels that thread of wire anchors his lineage
inside an ever-changing wind and is content.

---

[1] Gorgy was his father's favourite dog

About the Poem

Andrew reminded me that the dead live until memory's last word, and an unspoken person is unstitched of deed. This was slightly melancholic, definitely truthful and loaded with a deep sense of obligation. The first farmers fenced the boundary of their farms just as they fenced the boundary of their lives knowing it was part of their legacy. The son is constantly reminded of this when the wind frees their bones from the hills, the dog 'flocks the yards and the 'dust' men ghost the stables'. Reference to 'Hamlet's Kings' takes the idea further when herons feed on worms that have fed on Andrew's ancestors buried on the farm. These in turn fly in his eye keeping that legacy alive.

The last stanza returns to the main idea reminding readers that dead men's 'seed' left on battlefields is lineage 'unstitched' of deed. But it is Andy at the end of the poem who looks to the ridgeline where his ancestors first left their mark and is content in knowing he is anchored to the land and the legacy of his family lives on.

* * *

Like many of these men, Andrew's recall of his family history reflects his obligation to keep his past alive. His grandfather, Henry Parker Best had the third registered Romney Stud in New Zealand. His son Joe, fought through Sinai and Palestine with the Wellington Mounted Rifles during the First World War. While he was away, his brothers did not keep up the register which meant the stud was struck off.

In 1925, Joe decided he couldn't work with his brothers anymore and moved to a bush block at Pukengahu. [27] There he built a house and a herd of stud Romneys. Andrew and his wife, Claire, live there now.

Jack Best, Andrew's father, took over the farm from his father, Joe. During the Second World War, he served in the Merchant Navy.

Jack was a short lean muscular chap. He learnt he had a natural talent for boxing while in the Navy which was a way of protecting himself and keeping fit. Jack demonstrated his pugilist skills on occasions when Andrew's temper frayed on the farm. "You want to hit me? Come on then," Jack would tease. "Give it your best shot."

"Each time I threw a punch, he simply and easily ducked, swayed, tilted away and I'd receive a teasing light slap." Andy chuckled, "It was a good way for me to cool down and learn skill easily trumps youth."

"Ben Bishop and Dad had taught me to shear, I never thought I was a great shearer but in my early days, I challenged myself to shear two hundred in one day. Dad was rousing. I was struggling. The sheep were big and I was slipping further and further behind my schedule. What you don't do when that happens is fight the sheep which is what I began to do. A few I slapped over the nose and Dad said, 'When you finish fighting that one looks behind you.' Behind me were pens full of sheep. 'They're all waiting for you, boy and there's more outside. You'll never beat them if you're not smarter than them.' He was right of course. He had a really good temperament, never got stressed just mocked me when I did."

I thought I had one over him when it came to my ghetto blaster. Back in the day, I'd turn it up loud in the shed while shearing. Dad would come in and tell me to 'Turn that crap down!' That was the routine for years, turn the music up, get blasted by Dad to turn it down. Over time, the ghetto blaster got buggered, one speaker didn't work and the sound from the other was crackly. Dad came into the shed one day, and as usual, told me to turn it down or 'I'll put an axe through the bloody thing.'

Go on then, I replied, and I unplugged the stereo, wrenched it off the wall and threw it down onto the shearing shed floor. It smashed into thousands of pieces and I made out he had finally pushed me to my limits. Dad stared down at the detritus, then back up at me speechless. I was thinking, yes, I've finally got him. He didn't know the ghetto blaster was stuffed. Finally, he looked at me and said, that's the best management decision you have made in the last twenty years, boy. Andrew chuckled at the memory, "Bugger I thought, he still got me."

Jack took great pride in his farm and animals. He attended stock sales and agricultural shows throughout the country where he was well known and respected. Like most veterans, he had a strong moral compass even if it meant sometimes stepping close to the line to reinforce it.

Tales Told

One of Dad's highly prized pedigree rams was called Winston after WLS Churchill. Winston often demonstrated his desire to follow his namesake's adventures by finding ways to escape his paddock. With one eye serving himself and the other servicing the farm and having no concept of boundaries, Winston regularly searched for fresh pastures...and ewes.

On one occasion the neighbour, let's call him Bruce, caught Winston wandering down the road and took him back to his own yards where he painted him with blue raddle. That is a marker Stock Agents use when drafting sheep for the freezing works. A couple of days later at the local hydatid dog testing strip, Bruce arrived with Winston on the back of his Land Rover.

Dad was standing with a couple of local farmers when he saw his pedigree ram arrive dressed in blue. It was not something you did to another man's prized ram. Humiliating him might compromise his virility if he happened to glance at himself in a puddle. Disrespecting the owner was just as bad. Bruce was in no hurry to come over to talk after chaining his dogs to the testing strip. That gave Dad time to dart back to the Ute, grab a block of his own raddle and return to his mates. With the raddle held behind his back, he watched Bruce slowly wander over to the group of men. When questions were asked about the blue ram, he bluffed saying he'd found him like that. That's when Dad stepped forward, grabbed him by the hair and raddled the top of his head. Bruce stepped back, his face red, eyes flamed with anger ready to retaliate as Dad took up his pugilist stance and waited, expecting, but it never came.

Winston was repatriated with the ewes though they kept their distance until after rain.

* * *

"Jack was a humanist, carried no prejudice, judged character on work ethic and behaviour and didn't tolerate fools. I was thinking of joining the Navy and went to an interview. Several weeks later, I had not received any word from the recruitment officer regarding the meeting. When I broached the subject with Dad, he replied. 'Oh, he did ring, but I told him you weren't interested as our family had given enough to the forces.' Andy gave a thoughtful smile and added, 'He did things like that'."

"Dad was a special man. I think his war experience made him realise nothing in civilian life comes close to seeing people getting killed and mutilated around you, so why get stressed out when things go wrong, just enjoy every day you're alive.

He and I were working in the woolshed when this guy turned up wearing a suit and tie, polished shoes, a briefcase in one hand and a booklet in the other. He was a representative of a church. I was surprised Dad engaged with him, replying to the chap that he was happy with his spirituality. The church man replied that if he didn't believe in God not only, he, but his entire family would be condemned to a bottomless pit.

That statement piqued Dad's interest. 'A bottomless pit, you say?' Dad replied with a wry smile. 'Yes', for eternity.

'I'd have a bit of speed up, wouldn't I?'

I was only a teenager at the time and like the Jehovah man wasn't quite sure where Dad was going with this. In the silence, he continued, 'You'd only fall at a certain speed, right?'

The Jehovah man shrugged.

'But that would depend on whether your bottomless pit was subject to the laws of terminal velocity or not. So, is it?'

The church man gave a hesitant affirmation with a nod of his head. Dad could see his uncertainty and asked whether he knew what terminal velocity meant, which he didn't. Of course, Dad was more than happy to explain that a freefalling object only travelled as fast as its mass."

"This brings me to my point," said Dad as he stepped a little closer to the church man. "Would not freefalling into a bottomless pit be more pleasurable than spending an eternity with the likes of you?"

* * *

I was more than impressed with Dad. He was quick-witted and had acerbic wit which I was on the receiving end frequently like when I was learning to drive. I was heading into town with Dad as my passenger. The road was unsealed gravel. Suddenly Dad shouted, 'Shit, there's a pothole there and you missed it.'

I replied, 'That was my intention. I didn't want to hit it.'

"Well," he laughed, "you might as well turn around and get it because you've hit every other fucking one'."

Kevin 'Butch' Downs
Morori[28] – English

Image: Simeon Patience

Just Common Sense

Too many fellas sell once their olds have gone.
All that hard work for someone else to benefit from
just isn't right.
Then they fuck off to the city thinking
it's better than working the land
but that just isn't right.
Yah makes just the same money, probably
more on the land, it's not rocket science,
just got to know yah margins
otherwise, it just isn't right.
Yah screws the east coast farmer for grazing one year
and he's doing the same to you the next.
Yah just got to screw him harder
to get on top, it's not rocket science.
It's either in yah or not.
I reckon me granddaughter could just about run the farm,
she's three.
Gotta teaches kids early how to work.
Once they have a good work ethic, life's great.
It's not rocket science, been done for centuries.
Just common sense, but that's rare as hen's teeth these days,
isn't it?

About the Poem

This is a great example of colloquial language and a farmer's blunt, honest attitude and approach to life. He downplays his talent and skill as a very successful farmer by repeating the cliché 'it's not rocket science' and using the hyperbole his three-year-old granddaughter could run it. Maybe she could, after being brought up with a 'good work ethic'. Other cliches such as 'screw him harder' and 'rare as hen's teeth', the expletive 'fuck' and simple syntax anchor the man in a real world of hard work and integrity. There is little doubt that legacy will continue.

* * *

Kevin told me he only went to school to keep the Truancy Officer at bay. At fifteen years of age, he left and joined a shearing gang. He had been shearing since he was a 'little fella'. But it didn't take him long to realise there was more money in owning land and collecting the capital gain than shearing. His father, Burt, sold the farm to Kevin when he was twenty-one.

"He had faith in me. Gave me a break," said Kevin. "To own a farm that young was unusual in those days. Now the cost for a young fella to get land makes it all but impossible. I never really looked back after I purchased the farm. Roger Douglas [29] didn't make it easy in the early days. I bought the farm for four hundred thousand dollars and in two years, the value was almost halved and expenses rose by one-third, driven by interest rates of eighteen to twenty-one per cent. That was three times what I had been paying.

Now, each of my three children has their own farm and I'm setting up to provide for the next generation after them. Me wife, Jean and I have helped young fellas if they show they can work hard and are committed. Helped a few get a start on buying their own farms.

We shear around eighteen thousand ewes and carry four thousand stud Angus and Hereford cattle. What this family has achieved is on the back of dad's belief in me and we've never looked back. My parents knew I could work because they brought me up to do just that and we've passed that 'old way' of bringing kids up onto our children and grandchildren. When the grandchildren visit, they have their own named buckets at the back door. They collect them and go down and feed the chooks and collect the eggs, they help to feed out, they learn at an early age where their food comes from and that you must be responsible and commit to routines because animals are relying on you.

Eating at the table is the best way for families to communicate. Centuries back, it was probably a practical way to count off the kids to make sure none of them had been eaten or lost. Sitting in front of the television with your food on your lap robs you of that time to bond, and you know what, most people wouldn't know what they've lost."

* * *

A Tale Told

"It was 4.30 in the morning. We'd drunk a heap of rum 'cos I'd just bought a block of land at Strathmore. The commission was sixty-thousand dollars. The land agent was there. I said I'd fight him for the commission. I was going okay until he got me and flipped me right over. I had a brand-new pair of RM Williams boots worth four hundred dollars and my leg just snapped like a bloody carrot. I got my daughter to bring me home. She put me to bed. I couldn't get my boot off it was so tight. The ambulance picked me up at eight in the morning, the boys were still on the piss outside the hall, waved out at me as I passed. I was full of laughing gas, didn't feel a thing, brilliant. Ended up in the hospital. Now I have this hunk of metal in my leg."

"In the end, I didn't pay the commission, 'cos he felt guilty. He came and saw me in the hospital. Said we'd be even after what he'd done to my leg." Butch laughed. "I reckon it was worth it."

* * *

Remember that Robert Bly quote? When a child stands close to a father it gives the boy a certain confidence, an awareness, a knowledge of what it is to be male…You learnt from him. [2] For some, that comes from the raw, rough and tumble man; the unshaved, smelling of grass and soil bloke, the outdoor bloke with the odour of manual labour stained on his shirt; you know the barrel-chested grandfathers and fathers rolling and limping on buggered hips and knees, speaking in blunt coloured language.

Or, for others, it comes from the urban over-washed cliche, designer labelled, muscled and flexed by yoga and Pilates, speaking with the pastel-coloured language of neutrality (or surrender), drenched in commercial brands of aftershave, moisturisers and deodorants to become gender reduced and safe.

What about the father struggling to make ends meet, labouring on roads, digging trenches, lugging cables, tobacco or vape in his pocket, homemade tattoos on his arms or face, the follower of league or kickboxing, football or American Gridiron?

Stereotypes indeed. The question is which form of masculinity best serves the boy and the answer is they are all equally valid. The presence of the father to offer positive support and guidance is all that matters.

Roads. By Langley Herbert Pepperell.
Courtesy of Puke Ariki Library. PH 02011–2039

Kerry Turner
Cygnet, Tasmania, Australia

Image: Simeon Patience

John (Jack) Ernest Smith was brought up in a hard, cold hole in Tasmania, according to his son Kerry. "His father, my grandfather was illiterate but his mother, who was a teacher, taught Jack to read. He stayed around until his first marriage went 'belly up. He had to get out of there', so the family sent him up to the Northern Territory to find work. He ran out of money and telegrammed his father. It read: 'I'm broke (Stop) Walking.' (Stop) His old man sent back a telegram. 'Keep walking.' (Stop)."

When Dad came to New Zealand, he had only half a crown. He worked timber up in Northland then down to Bennydale and into the timber trail, which extended right up into Aupouri, Pureora and Ongarue [30]. There was so much timber; they reckon 700,000 cubic feet per year was removed over fifteen years.

Dad ended up managing the Moki Road Mill. [31] He married Louise McCarty, who was the local postmistress and bought a farm at Kahuratahi. He was an axe man and loved trout fishing.

I loved the old man—out of respect, I suppose the way he treated others, supported and encouraged all his children. Understood politics. Jack told us boys when Muldoon got into power, 'You guys are in trouble. Keep your affairs in order, pay your bills. Be sensible'.

Listening to Kerry, I got the impression Jack encouraged his children to take responsibility for giving their lives meaning, to shape them through their endeavours.

"Dad refinanced to buy a farm for my eldest brother, then refinanced again to buy a farm for my elder sister. He bought this farm for me and another for my younger brother. My younger sister didn't want a farm, so he financed her into a house in New Plymouth. Dad had faith in his children and invested in them. When he died, he did not have millions in his account, but everyone was happy, you can't ask for more than that.

He never hit us but was stern. He was a man's man.

One Sunday night when I was twelve, Dad took me to a western movie in town. They always played Westerns on Sunday. It was a special moment, just me and him. It was wonderful. I suppose it might have been because I was a sickly kid. I was held back two years at school because of it. Dad got me to read comics, westerns were particularly popular back then which helped with my reading.

He was a fly fisherman. He had a caravan at Taupo. He liked his solitude at times. I caught my first trout with him. I dropped the rod and pulled it in by hand, I was so excited. He wasn't good with dogs. When mustering, he used the 'b' word a lot but he wasn't saying bastard, he was saying, 'You passed it. You passed it.' The only way he could get his dogs to 'GET IN BEHIND!' was to turn his back on them.

People respected my dad. He was a top farmer. Jack loved his land. He had a big vegie garden so we were totally self-sufficient. We grew so much that we sold Rhubarb and sacks of potatoes to the vegetable shop in town.

He had been a crook for a while. In the cupboard of his hospital room, he had three bottles of whisky ranked on quality. Matron said, 'Which one you got depended on how much he liked you.' Matron like his close mates got the best.

I was with him when he died. Early in the morning, he was sitting in bed and he just rolled over put his arm around Lois (mum) and passed. We sat there for half an hour before I went and got the Matron.

Kerry told me he shares his mother's love of music. Her brother, Ron McCarty had been at Monte Casino and returned from the Second World War with shell shock (PTSD). Jack Turner, like so many of the older generation supported the war veterans.

"I remember having to go and fill up Ron's wood box and do chores like that. Dad would visit him for a chat. He'd been pretty knocked around."

Wood Cutters by George Herbert
Courtesy of Puke Ariki PHO2013–0004

Exotic Dancers

Out here everything is green.
Green is a beautiful colour but so monotonous
until dock snuck in on jerseys and socks
in pockets and sacks in 1832.

Those exotic dancers bullied the soil,
pushed against the sun to dance the warm wind wild.
Salomes, tall and veiled dance in the sunlight
rising in reds and browns against the flat low green
teasing the wind and sun to strip them bare
to ravage them dry.

Fences cannot hold these Hebrew dancers
who age and wither and buckle
against the fetlock of stock to sneak away
as seed on wool, belly and bird and rise again
long after our fences and houses, machines
and footprints, memories and children have gone.

About the Poem

The exotic weed with its 'tall and veiled' reds and browns is called dock. The plant is described as 'Salome' a Hebrew word meaning 'peace'. Ironically, it was also the name of a Jewish princess who instigated the execution of John the Baptist. Her dancing pleased Emperor Herod Antipas so much he offered to accept any request she made. Salome's mother insisted she asked for John's head on a plate.

Although dock will 'age and wither and buckle', each season their seeds will rise again the following year to entice the sun and wind to strip them bare. It is ironic that something so basic will outlive humanity with all its sophistication. Interesting to apply the definition of 'weed' to each.

Abandoned House and Dock

Colin (Collie) Hancock
Mow Cop, England

Image: Simeon Patience

One + One

Collie's grandfather Peter left Mow Cop, Staffordshire and sailed to New Zealand in 1880. He brought with him his revivalist god and new bride Emma who played piano at church. They were part of a group that broke away from traditional Methodists called the Primitive Methodists. Hugh Bourne established it in Mow Cop at the beginning of the nineteenth century. Bourne set up large outdoor meetings to attract everyone, rich and poor to worship together. Many Methodists had felt the original church was elitist with many middle- and upper-class members not happy to worship alongside farmers, miners and quarrymen.

Peter Hancock was a quarryman.

Grandfather Peter worked for New Zealand Rail. He laid quarry rock under the tracks because he knew big things needed small things to move. "As a quarry worker back in England, he learnt to judge stone. If you look at the rock under our railway, you'll see it's all the same colour and size and that rock is hard," Collie told me.

"Dad learnt about rock from his dad. Sometimes I'd go with him when he was breaking stone to fill in gateways on the farm. He'd give me a wee hammer and he'd have a big one and we'd bash away together."

When Collie was young and nippy as a trout tickled pink, he remembers his father as Saturday's wing forward, MC welcoming them back from the war, butcher, farmer, husband, father and a god-fearing Methodist to boot. "I watched him at dances, dance like a feather, wondering how a twenty-stone man could move with such a light step."

When Collie was happy as a new boy in the schoolyard playing, life tumbled never-ending-down-round mountain rock through the farm where his father and mother worked. He helped his dad clear the bush with a cross-cut saw. "Dad cleared a hell of a lot of bushes under Mount Egmont," which was taller than his dad was wide and their land never wider than with bush inside. "I remember straddling to a split our horse called Monty and learning big things could move with just a wee kick.

One day, Sister John asked each pupil in our class what they had for breakfast. This was during the late 1930s. When she asked me, I told her I had a trout and everyone else in the family had a trout too. She was very surprised, frowned in disbelief and moved on to ask the next pupil. After church on Sunday, we were all in the car ready to leave when Sister John trotted over to Mum's window. 'Mrs Hancock,' she began. 'Colin tells me he had a trout for breakfast the other morning.' Mum confirmed I had and added that we had eight trout for breakfast because Dad had caught that many the night before. Sister John simply huffed and nodded. We had no refrigeration so they had to be eaten. Dad used a hoop iron to stun trout as he waded up the river."

When Collie was happy playing rugby 'gainst girls eyes watching, his father changed direction with a silent and sudden step. His big heart stopped at fifty-five in nineteen-forty-four. Collie's older brother Gordon came back from the war the following year but did not want to work on the farm for a wage of three pounds a week. Collie left school at fourteen to work the tilted farm to right the loss of his father. What he had learnt from his father by that age, he applied to his new role. His mother was always there to support and advise. "Back then, most boys left school at fifteen because they had jobs or apprenticeships lined up. Today you still have kids down at the school at eighteen with little or no direction. I had fifty-five cows to milk and two acres of whitey wood left to clear." With his four-foot handsaw, he cut it all down, having learnt from his father one tree eventually adds up to all. Over the three months the cows were not milked, he built a new milking shed using only a hammer, level and axe. "I mixed concrete, learnt to plaster the shed walls, and dug the pit by hand. Today it would take three months just to get a building consent."

Over the following years, Collie used his horses Monty and Bonnie to haul rock from the river. "If I couldn't get the rock onto the sledge, I'd either leave it or nap it in the river. I lined the side of the race with the rocks." In winter, after he had fed hay out to the cows, Collie napped rock for a new race that covered his winter heart. Tap, tap, tap went the four-pound hammer because he knew one piece eventually added up to all.

When he was a young man with smiles on his peddles, Collie biked to dances in town and at twenty he borrowed his mother's car to court Cecelia. That was when he realised one plus one can make one.

Now he's old and happy as an armchair rocking in a hay paddock fresh with grass, and his dusty eyes mutter how his love has left but he can count off his knee generations of progeny, knowing one true love lives forever.

Nothing else to do but work…always had something to do. Filled in life making small differences. Each generation makes the next generation a little easier…I've had a very lucky life.

Collie Hancock

Colin Wheeler
Tainui,[32] Polish

Image: Simeon Patience

"My mother and father struggled to make ends meet but Dad's massive garden helped. There were big sections in town in those days. Any surplus carrots and potatoes we had could feed half the neighbours. Even after a hard day's work, Dad would come home, have a cup of tea and then he would be out in the dark doing the garden. He died of a heart attack at seventy-six. Mum lived to be ninety-two. She would have lived a lot longer if she had looked after herself. The woman was never sick. Mum made all our clothes. Like most women and some men in those days, knitting and sowing was a way to save money. Flour bags were the lining of our clothes. A little flap was made for the zip in our shorts. Mum and Dad couldn't afford to buy us shoes so what Dad did was cut an old car tyre into the shape of our feet, the tyres were pretty thin in those days then we strapped them on, a pair would last forever.

Mum and Dad taught us to be resilient, to think outside the box to find solutions and to also give back to the community. I was the president of the golf club seniors and veterans, the racing club, and indoor bowls. My brother Clive gave a huge amount of his time to the swimming club as a coach and custodian.

Most of my life, I was in sales. Started travelling around selling frozen peas before they were 'free-flow'. That was all there was in the way of frozen food. In a few years, I was selling frozen meat that was produced in town, sausages by the dozens, bags of vegetables, Peter Pan ice cream. Twenty-kilogram cartons of fish came up from Tullies in Motueka. Sold cartons of mutton birds to a select type who liked them. I certainly didn't. Initially, I had a small truck, but it became bigger and bigger very quickly. I'd add everything up in my head, recorded as I went. Sold off the truck around South Taranaki, Opunake, Awatuia, Urenui, Waitara, Inglewood, it was a huge area to cover. The roads were atrocious. Out in the 'back country', McCarty's bulldozer would be called in to open the road after a slip so the truck could get through to Tahora and Whangamomona. All the farmers out there knew what time the truck was coming so they stayed off the road until I'd passed. Driving out there was hard on the nerves. I had a few close calls with cars but I was bigger than a car so the car would end up in the drain, not me. I always carried a rope to pull them out.

The farmers' wives were great hosts," Colin said. "At the end of the day, I'd felt like a teapot. Everywhere I went, there would be a cup of tea, scone or sponge cake waiting. Don was the chef at Te Wera, I'd have a cuppa there and eel was always on the menu. Then I'd stop at Whangamomona and there'd be a cuppa and cake there…rude not to eat it. At Kahuratahi, another cup of tea would be waiting.

I was the first driver selling frozen peas. Farmers wanted bigger packets, so my boss, Mr Gordon McCutcheon, called James Wattie [33] and asked him to make bigger sizes for farmers. That's when they moved from solid packs to free flow. There were no frozen chickens in the nineteen fifties. No poultry at all. McCutcheon built an abattoir and canvased chicken farmers for the product. We would pick up poultry from their gates and bring them into the shed where a guy called Terry Lovell hung them from little metal funnels. With the chicken's neck exposed, Terry would walk along and slit each in turn. He was very quick and efficient.

At night, the plucking and gutting staff came in. Once clean, the chickens were dropped into vats of cold water. Next morning out of the water, they'd come and be packed into bags that were peddled sealed, and frozen. Any damaged ones were put into boxes for hotels.

Mr McCutcheon got to a point where he needed a decent freezer. He had to borrow from the bank to build it. After five years, he called me into his office one day and said we needed to celebrate because all his equipment, including the freezer, was freehold. No one envisaged frozen foods would become so big. [34]

Then there were crayfish. Coal sacks of them came over from Opunake on a truck called the 'flea.' Twenty sacks with twenty crays in each. All had to be cooked. I hated crayfish but had to cook them dressed in knee-high gumboots, a full rubber apron and large gloves. We cooked the first grade first and worked our way down. All done in a steam cleaner. We plugged the bottom and put wet sacks on the top. Once cooked they were frozen and sold like hotcakes. Those were great times," Colin said with a spark in his eye. "Interesting and exciting when you had to think outside the box to get things done.

Dad instilled in us how to work hard. Nothing came easy. You learnt the value of money because no one had much of it in the Depression and you had to earn it before you could spend it. Dad taught us to mow lawns, cut hedges and stack firewood, there were always chores and you were expected to do them. He was up at the crack of dawn and back at night when we were in bed, so we didn't see much of him because in those days, you were in bed by seven o'clock."

Image: Simeon Patience. East from Strathmore Saddle.

Brett Sangster
Peterhead, Scotland

Image: Joanna Piatek

Brett's great-grandfather George was born at Slains, Aberdeenshire in 1859. He tossed a coin on the wharf at Peterhead in 1880 to decide whether he'd emigrate to New Zealand or Canada. He was ferried onto a Timaru beach in New Zealand by longboat that same year.

George was a stonemason and worked on the bridge abutments for the now submerged bridge at Cromwell. From there, he travelled to Invercargill where he built stone houses and married Ann Glendinning Ingles in 1890.

George came to Stratford for work. He bought a farm, became Mayor for a short spell in the early 1900s and between him and Ann they had seventeen children. George was asked how they went about naming all their children and he replied with a smile, "I began with Adam, as he was the first." Adam was born in Westport.

The following is an abridgement of Brett's written account of his grandfather, Adam.

* * *

Grandpa told of his exploits during the First World War, fighting Turks at Gallipoli and in Palestine, Home Guard duties during World War Two, farming experiences, rifle marksmanship, lawn bowls, livestock, bureaucracy, the bloody royal family, explosives, lawn culture, neighbours, motorcycle riding, literature, politics and bagpipe playing.

He was widely read. Bertrand Russell's autobiography and Shakespeare's plays were read for pleasure. I think he became an atheist after reading the Bible.

He told me many of his wartime experiences; when he grew a beard but shaved it off when the crickets in it kept him awake at night, or the plagues of blowflies at Gallipoli in no-man's-land, and his admiration for a Turkish sniper in Palestine, who shot him. What should have been a bullet through his heart was absorbed by his ammunition bandolier "Great shot," Grandpa said. "At three hundred yards with less than three seconds to make it."

"Like most farmers in the day, Grandpa was able to wander into Newton King's stock and station store and buy gelignite, detonators and rolls of fuse. He had no qualifications, just heaps of 'experience' so he knew how to make things go bang but usually with a bit too much bang. Stories of him disposing of the corpses of large animals and depositing a large stump on the roof of the house were legendary."

As more and more regulations are applied to traditional handcrafts such as making cheese, butchering sheep or beef, building a shed, laying concrete and digging drains, the value of those skills devalues to a point where they are no longer used and possibly lost.

While we are made up of combinations of our parents' genetics, how a person develops socially is more likely to be shaped by the family dynamic rather than a code inscribed on their chromosomes.

Households founded on understanding the value of hard work and community service produced offspring with the same values.

"Adam's father, George Arthur Sangster was Mayor of Stratford and his wife's father, John Bird Hine was Member of Parliament for Stratford and a Cabinet Minister.

I believe Grandpa's experiences during the First World War at Gallipoli and in Palestine contributed to his lack of religious belief. He only went to church for important events like weddings and funerals and catching up with friends. He wasn't an evangelical atheist and let others close to him practice whatever belief system they wished. Those actions taught me what faith truly is. This background also shaped my dad's development.

My dad, Robert went to church with his mother, married at an Anglican church, and was the Eltham Parish's representative at the Anglican General Synod. However, Dad never really talked about his personal religious beliefs. He taught me that people will judge you more by your actions than your words.

Both Mum and Dad liked to read. Dad's preference was anything with a ripping yarn whether fiction or non-fiction, preferably with a strong hero character like Ed Hillary, Chuck Yeager or Ben Hogan. He also devoured journals like farming magazines. They were both interested in what I was reading, which was always followed by the challenge of summarising it in a sentence.

Grandpa appreciated the value of strong relationships. On our wedding day, he told Jane, my wife, and I to never take each other for granted."

Brett Sangster

A Tale Told

When Adam Sangster and his wife Madge moved into town, I was often asked to mow their lawns. They were secured inside narrow concrete edges, fertilised, weedless and uniform. He instructed me on how to mow them, which had to be east to west in straight lines, not too fast or too slow. I had to arrive after the dew had lifted and not arrive at all if the grass was wet. He always checked the mower was set to the correct height, the oil and petrol were at acceptable levels, and the catcher was clean and attached.

As a young boy, I mowed them in a quick reckless fashion, believing they were only grass. Once the mower stopped, Uncle Ad was at the back door of the house leaning on his walking stick. In hindsight, I think he must have timed me. Down the steps, he would come and slowly step across the lawn inspecting as he went. Any shake of his head or tut-tut indicated he had seen sloppy workmanship which meant the mower was retrieved and with the point of his cane I would have to cut a tuft of grass here and a blade there. Very quickly, I learnt his motto, 'Do things once, and do them right.' I also learnt lawns were more than just grass.'

* * *

This type of intergenerational legacy is dwindling fast. How many of us still have parents or grandparents who lived through a war or the Depression, pioneered a new land, enjoyed a night out without consuming alcohol or drugs, or made and wore homemade clothes? There is more than a hint of truth in the words of Mustapha Mond in Huxley's Brave New World when he said, 'stability isn't nearly so spectacular as instability. And being contented has none of the glamour of a good fight against misfortune, none of the picturesqueness of a struggle with temptation, or a fatal overthrow by passion or doubt. Happiness is never grand.'

There is some truth in these words. Is it not said that the greatest reward comes from the greatest endeavour? Maybe the easiest and safest way to find this these days is on a game console or to live vicariously through a character in a movie for a few hours. Is life becoming more and more of an escape where the qualities and values respected and required in the past have less or no value?

There is more to grass than just grass, right?

Road and Trees by Eliot Millar King.
Courtesy of Puke Ariki PH020150150

Donald Alexander Spottiswood Hopkirk
Melrose, Roxburghshire, Scotland

Image: Jo Stallard. Chalk and Charcoal

"My religion is in the hills. The high country speaks to me."

Don's father, John (Jack) Joseph Hopkirk was born in 1898 in Scotland. He immigrated at the age of seventeen to follow his dream of going farming. Jack laboured on farms in the Waikato and Waverly before his father purchased a farm at Makahu in Eastern Taranaki. "It was so far away from civilisation," Don laughed, "it was probably the cheapest piece of land in the country." The land was hilly, mostly bush and rough. Logs and stumps that hadn't burnt during the initial clearing still had to be removed. "Stumping was a hard labour-intensive job. They would dig deep around the stump, attach chains and hitch them to horses or bullocks."

'Eruptite' was the name of a popular explosive used at the time. A stubborn stump didn't stand a chance with these explosives packed tightly beneath it. Dad's sister-in-law was pushing her newborn along the road on one particular occasion when the fuse had been lit. She was over the gully and across a paddock when the explosion occurred. Wood and dirt flew up in the air clearing the stump with so much force that one large piece of wood dropped just in front of the pram. Dad's sister-in-law turned around smartly and went back to the house. We're getting out of here, she said to her husband, before that lunatic brother of yours kills us.

'They did.' Don chuckled. 'They move to Hamilton'.

Don's father had limited skills when he started farming but as Don said, Needs must. That was the motto and they quickly developed. The small house expanded with each child as the need for a bigger and better kitchen, laundry and inside toilet were required. "There was no such thing as can't. You had to learn as you went along. You wouldn't have survived if you didn't. That was an important lesson I learnt from Dad.

He always said, 'If I can clear enough land for one thousand ewes, I'll be right. But as he cleared the bush, he needed twelve hundred then fifteen hundred, then eighteen hundred ewes.

Education was important to our family, Mum in particular. The Catholic church had come up from Wellington to gauge how many people would support a new school if it was built there. Mrs Celia Hopkirk promised, 'If you build it, I'll send a boy'." That boy was Don.

He left home for Silverstream College at the age of twelve. He counted his days at school as being 'lucky'. "It was a great experience. I particularly enjoyed commerce which served me well when I eventually moved onto the farm." Education 'rounded' him he said. "It broadened my horizons. I met and have stayed in touch with so many interesting people." Don, in turn, sent his son William to the same school.

Don told me an Irish chap, fresh off the boat had been employed to maintain the roads with a wheelbarrow and shovel out at Makahu. His name was Tammy. "When Dad told him on the day he lined up with the Wellington Mounted rifles with his horse ready to get on the troop ship, the First World War ended. Tammy was delighted and said in the broadest Irish accent, 'Well, I'll be buggered, missed the war. You're the luckiest man I've ever met!' Then Dad told him that when the influenza epidemic hit Trentham Military base when he was there, he never caught it. Tammy was flabbergasted and said, 'Well, I'll be buggered missed the influenza too! Christ, you're the luckiest man I ever met, best to stay around you just in case a bit drops off'."

Don worked with his father from the age of twenty-one. Eventually, all three of Celia and Jack's boys worked on the farm during some part of their early lives picking up valuable skills and experience. "Dad became a sort of director after that," laughed Don. "With his free time, he and Mum worked in their garden. They both loved gardening." Don's brother, Jim had the same passion, gaining national and international acclaim for his garden which was next to the farm.

Don was teased when he returned to the farm after living in Wellington. "It took a while to shed the 'city-slicker' label the locals called me." An opportunity to prove himself came during spring. Back before top-dressers, fertiliser was only applied to the flats using horse and sledge. This meant the hills starved. "There was an area of flat land high up on a hill which had never been fertilised," Don told me. "I was determined to prove my worth when the men employed to spread it said they would spread the fertiliser on the high paddock if my brother and I brought it up to them. We halved this 150–pound bag of fertiliser and carried it up the hill.

Dad was keen on wool before prices boomed in the fifties. He had created a small stud of his own and was always looking to improve productivity and advance in all aspects of farming." Don told me he thought his 'dad was a couple of steps ahead of other farmers.' Like his father, Don had great foresight. He held Directorships of meat companies that set standards for the direction of farming which he also applied to his own.

Four of his and Celia's five children were daughters. The Hopkirk's were well in advance of gender equality as all children worked on the farm while being encouraged to investigate and push boundaries with an inquiring mind. That was reflected in some of them writing for science and farming magazines, often promoting cutting-edge ideas and innovation.

"My father's brother was killed in France," Don told me. "He was a lieutenant. He had survived Gallipoli and was in France in 1916. A German sniper had been bothering his section along the trench. Witnesses said he had popped his head up for a second or two to gauge the position of the sniper and was shot." Don paused lost in thought then lifted his head and said, "You learn fairly quickly as a boy, when you hear accounts like that, to appreciate family and to appreciate what you have."

Peter Bayly
Devon, Cornwell

Image: Simeon Patience

Fifteen Bailys disembarked from the ship Amelia Thompson at Moturoa on 25 March 1841. They were part of one hundred and eighty-seven Devonshire emigrants that left London. It took five and a half months at sea before they anchored on the 3rd of September. The rough sea meant passengers had to remain onboard until conditions were safe enough for them to be transported to Moturoa Beach on 5 September.

'Yeoman' and 'Agricultural Labourer' described the Bayly men on the passenger list. They were part of a family that ranged in age from one month old, Isaac, to thirty-six-year-old Thomas.

Bailys settled in North Taranaki, some in the south and others travelled to Hawkes Bay on the east coast where they developed seventeen-thousand-eight hundred hectares into grazing for sheep, beef and stud bulls. One of the Bayly men fought alongside Gustavus Ferdinand von Tempsky [35] in the New Zealand Forest Rangers. Cape Egmont Lighthouse can be found at the end of Bayly Road around the coast of New Plymouth. The road is named after the fourth Lighthouse Keeper.

The family's memory of leaving their home country and enduring an arduous voyage strengthened their resolve to make a go of it. "Dad had faith in us to make a go of farming," Peter told me. "If we didn't, we knew he'd kick our asses, so you didn't do anything by halves. You gave it your best all the time."

Evan David Bayly (Taffy) with his new wife Hilda worked hard to finally purchase their dairy farm in 1950. Their first job was milking forty cows and looking after one hundred pigs and crops on what was known as the Binnie Estate. His father, Eric, had little faith in Taff's decision to buy the farm. "Pop never stepped foot on dad's farm," said Peter. "They didn't have a good relationship. I remember Dad taking the chainsaw down to Pop to get sharpened and within minutes I'd hear voices raised. They were too alike." A father's 'doubt' in a son could harden the young man's determination to prove the father wrong. Taffy took the bit between his teeth to do just that and later, his son Peter would do the same. "Dad reluctantly made the decision when he bought the farm to sell a top horse called 'Taffy' and put the money into buying fertiliser and water troughs which paid off. The farm's production more than trebled the first year and then improved on that in the second."

Listening to Peter, you could get a sense of his father's need to get things right, particularly when continually challenged by a doubting father. "I learnt early on to form an opinion and stick by it. That stemmed from Dad. He was so opinionated you never went into battle with him without doing your homework. He was very thorough. I admired that about him, he was always fricking right, which was incredibly frustrating." Peter has passed this on to his children. "It's too easy for children to sit back and be disinterested particularly in things that directly affect them such as politics. You need to have a voice. We'd have family gatherings and before long fists would be thumping the table and voices animated but the language would be articulate, forceful and clear. If you had an opinion in the Bayly family you let people know."

When Taff's boys were about to leave school, he made it quite clear that they needed to go off and learn another man's trade. "My brother Roger went off and trained as a mechanic and I loved banging in nails so became a carpenter. We did that for nine years before coming back onto the farm as 50/50 share milkers. Dad implied it was our choice but when I think about it, I don't think we had a choice at all."

Teenagers like Peter and Roger who had chosen trades out of school not only gained invaluable skills from the men they worked with but within that microcosm, they learnt the structure of the broader social order. The apprentice initially learnt their place beginning with menial jobs like being the 'gofer', while learning to listen and show respect for those more skilled and older. It was a natural way for the young to develop their sense of place within a social hierarchy. As they advanced with age and knowledge those values would be passed on to the new apprentices.

His boss, Buzz Web crafted the work ethic Peter brought to the job. "Buzz taught me to work smarter by apportioning time, to focus it on more important details and less on the rudimentary jobs. He was an important influence during those years I worked off the farm. You don't realise how much you influence young lives. I was a rugby coach, now I have these men coming up to me and telling me how important I was when they were growing up. It makes you proud to think you were a role model."

Taffy Bayly's passions were a split between the farm and harness racing. He dedicated most of his life to serving the club which was formed in 1958. Later his service was recognised when he became a life member. Peter continued that community service, giving seven years to the local Pembroke School Board and ten years to the Agricultural and Pastural Show Committee. Giving back to the community is to be part of it. It seems to be less of a 'chore' for rural people to donate their time when the fabric of their health and well-being relies upon their local communities.

"I wouldn't say I loved my father. He was a bloody hard man to love. But shit, I respected him. His judgement of livestock was second to none. I used to marvel at the details he could pick up in an animal. I respected his honesty, integrity and fairness but being in the same paddock as him was impossible because he knew everything and he never held back if you didn't do it his way. He never held back telling Bev, that's my wife, what he thought of Roger and my farming skills. They're a pair of useless bastards. They'll go broke! I should take the farm off them!"

Of course, down at the racecourse, it was a different matter telling everyone that would listen, 'Those boys are doing bloody well, proud of them.' But he never told you…well, not until just before he died. One sentence of acknowledgement was all it took to wipe away all the harsh words he had said, all the misbelief I thought he might have carried. 'You've done a good job on the farm, boy.'

"We grow up wanting to please our fathers and to be like them in certain ways but be better versions. 'I can say that about my son,' said Peter. 'He's a much better version of me. I'm so proud of him'."

"Do you tell him that?"

"What do you think?" Peter replied with a hefty laugh.

Hass Herbert
Bath, England

Image: Simeon Patience

A Tale Told

Young heading dog bounds to no whistle, eager to smudge talk about timber and sheep, dry stock and hills as old men still love timberless pasture. Top-dressers whistle through their teeth as they mutter 'bout extraordinariness of machines, their hands take off from tabletop airstrips flying through the air. They talk 'bout 'widow makers' cracking and splitting, 'bout trees slipping down the shaft, 'bout the blokes that didn't get away.

    They loved long-wheelbase Dodges, six cylinders, a devil of a job getting to town across shingle and mud, rain-drowning holes gasping for air and roads that could open the belly of a car. They talk steam trains, freight, and passenger, how they knew the driver by the sound of the engine, 'bout newspaper headlines of war and the Great Depression.

    They're drinking gin but talk homebrew and dandelion wine, how Mrs Shewry smashed the keg in 1939. So prim and proper, she wasn't having a repeat of inebriated blokes on the shed floor. They argue about politics, not sides but degree, how quickly, or not, things should move. They talk in spells charming time on the mantelpiece clock, about dusting the breaks and eight wire fences, windows to the future pinned into cushions of dirt, about pigs bloated with lambs. They say the young fella's a hard case. They say Hass's a chip off two old blocks, that he's tough, courageous and mad, fifth generation and all that. And he tells them about GPS explaining the acronym. About working on oil rigs and working white-collar in Melbourne. With a glint in his eye, he talks about Facebook, tinder and women in America and Sydney and Melbourne and Denmark and Asia, about falling and leaping from aeroplanes and lifting on strings like dandelion wine, about somersaults and back flips, about Bungie and parachutes folded and bagged like the value of shares and the price of gold. He reads and listens not to fools or liberal opinions if hard work and common sense are not at their base. He discerns outcomes like the weather by looking at clouds, a practical yet seemingly simple talent for someone fast-moving below.

* * *

Hass's great-great-grandfather arrived in 1854 and moved to Hawkes Bay. Herbertville was named after the family. Hass's grandfather Mick came to Eastern Taranaki after numerous labouring jobs.

As a little fella before and after primary school, Mick hand-milked sixty cows. Family history goes that his mother was an artist who was eccentric. Mick would get so cold in the house that he'd climb out his window and sleep with the dog in his kennel. His sister would do the same, but she caught hydatids and died.

At fourteen years old, Mick worked at a sheep station. He was constantly damp as his clothes would never dry in the hut. He was fed leftovers, worked like a horse, and paid fifteen shillings a week. There were twenty shillings to the pre-decimal pound at that time. Despite the hard living conditions and work, Mick gained skills that would put him in good stead for the future.

At sixteen years old, Mick was living in a twelve by ten-foot hut with a dirt floor and three other men. He worked on other stations for four further years in similar conditions, learning fencing, scrub cutting, maintaining his axes and saws and basic animal husbandry. Out of necessity, he also learnt to cook, wash, and darn his clothes. [36]

Mick was married when he moved to Kahuratahi to manage a farm. When he left that position in 1911, he purchased twelve hundred acres with a heart Totara homestead on it. That house had belonged to Ned Shewry who had twice been crowned world champion axeman. Hass lives in that house today.

Mick Herbert worked. He knew the measure of a man was based on that tenet. Pneumonia kept him from going to the war but it never stopped him from doing a hard day's work. The local power board put up for tender a contract to clear a chain of bush on either side of where the powerlines were to be placed. Mick won the tender. The power board believed he had a gang of men working for him but they were wrong it was just Mick but he fulfilled the contract on time.

Hass is rooted in that tradition with a strong moral compass and a commitment to what he believes is right. Independent, astute, and resourceful he represents the continuation of the 'genuine' rural bloke with the additional layers of education, travel and a white-collar job in the city can bring.

"I worked for the family business in Melbourne," he told me. "GPS, that sort of thing. Said I'd give it a year if I didn't like it, I'd bugger off. I didn't like it and stayed for eight. I converted an ambulance to live in. Sold that and bought a seven-metre Sprinter from a plumber. That gave me a little more comfort and room. The plumber left all his signwriting on it. I took off the phone numbers and left the rest so it didn't look like it was worth robbing. It was cheaper than renting a place just to hang my clothes. If I wasn't working, I'd be hunting or parachuting or diving and there were ways of getting a parking permit for a street without paying. The more obvious you are the less notice they take, particularly if you're a plumber. You don't want to get offside with a plumber. Hard enough to find one as it is."

A Tale Continued…

Outside the pub old fellas sup their beer talking 'bout foreigners buying up good land to plant Radiata. They say over seventeen thousand hectares of exotics have been planted since 2013 and speculate on how dry stock numbers have dropped, and the record price of beef up to seven dollars and thirty cents a kilo. They talk emissions and legislation about that young Hass fella with his Aerokopter skimming over hilltops the extraordinariness of Leonardo at drawing one and Bruce Herbert's shearing tally still on the Kahuratahi shed wall, four hundred and seven in one day.

* * *

I, Woke

Often, I remind myself hills
are mummified sheep dulled
by prevailing winds because
heart is too accepting of
what the eye is told.
Sometimes, heart is painted
with bruises yellow, green and blue
because it must feel what it's told is true.
You see my back's become a stretcher,
a gurney for hills covered with battens
and wires and strainers, preventing dust
from slipping into a question carried on the wind.

Sometimes, I dream in multiple
languages in several different
shapes not knowing which is trending
what to fret important.
Unsure who I'm supposed to be
I climb on fences, my feet slide
along the lowest wire fearing
the ever-changing climate,
below,
hoofing the thin soil
they tell me there is nothing to fear,
they tell me, let go we've got you;
they tell me they care.
But I know the faceless won't hold-true,
better to dream and dust in flight
than wither fenced on a hill in plain sigh.

About the Poem

World Wars and the Great Depression affirmed a country's sovereignty. People rallied together to assert shared values in a bid to unify and stay strong. Memories of those times have all but gone leaving a reduced sense of who or what we are as identities and cultures continue to blur. The theme of 'I Woke' is in the multiple meanings of 'woke', the most basic is waking from sleep. The other 'woke' is more complex to define. It can be positive and negative depending on an individual's stand on a subject. In the poem, it refers to the fear and confusion the speaker feels over what and who they should be.

The speaker is aware that the heart is too accepting of what the eye is told. In other words, one must be cautious of how one looks and what to think and speak in order to 'fit' in. The hills symbolise people who comply. They are 'mummified sheep' and the 'battens and wires and strainers' hold them in place. They are fenced by their conformity and acceptance that the 'faceless' will look after them.

The speaker is anxious and 'frets' to understand what is important and where to stand in relation to 'society'. Choosing the lowest wire to stand on reveals the speaker has little doubt falling is inevitable and knows the distance to the ground from there is the shortest. Despite reassurance by the 'faceless' that 'they care', the speaker would rather 'dream and dust in flight' than be fenced like a sheep on a hill.

The Icarus analogy is effective. It identifies the speaker as young and prepared to challenge authority and test boundaries rather than be fenced by society's 'wokeness'.

Colin MacFarlane
Finnart, Scottish Highland

Image: Mark Bellringer

Roy MacFarlane had three boys Jimmy, Rodney and Colin. Roy was a prisoner of war for three years after being captured in Crete in 1941. Two thousand one hundred and eighty other New Zealand soldiers were captured at the same time. That was the largest number of New Zealand POWs ever taken in a single battle. "Roy was a quiet man," said Colin. "He never talked about the war. He could have been shot in the leg for all the family knew. He was initially held in an overcrowded transit camp near Galatas. Prisoners suffered through a lack of food and medicine, shocking sanitation and disease. Dysentery was rife."

'If you soiled your clothes, all you could do was go down to the beach and get in the tide.' [37]

The prisoners were transported by train to camps such as Stalag VIII-B, later renumbered Stalag-344. This Stalag was near Lambsdorff (now Lambinowice) in Silesia. As the Red Army advance began in January 1945 the Nazis force marched eighty-thousand allied prisoners in groups of two to three hundred westward across Poland, Czechoslovakia and Germany to escape the Russians. These were known as Death Marches. Many men died from the cold when temperatures dropped as low as minus twenty-five. Those who lagged or were too ill to walk were shot. The march covered around nine hundred and sixty-two kilometres.

"I was told the war changed Roy. He had been a great swimmer and golfer. He and his mate made the first surfboard out of wood. It was so bloody heavy it took three of them to carry it to the surf." Colin told me his father 'saved eight out of twelve people at Fitzroy beach one summer when they had been swept out to sea in a rip.' That was the beach where Roy taught his boys how to swim. "Roy took one of us under each arm and waded out beyond the waves and let us go. You either sank or swam. He followed as we frantically doggy-paddled to the beach. Then he'd pick us up, turn around and take us out again." Colin chuckled. 'That's how you quickly learnt to swim.'

"I remember him sitting in his chair in the lounge reading the newspaper, drinking tea and smoking his flake tobacco rollie. He made his smoke so thick the two papers just touched. They were thick as a cigar. I liked the smell of it but hated the smell of the commercial brand Mum smoked. Early evening we'd be sitting down watching Hogan's Heroes and he'd be chuckling away. We asked him if that was like the camp he was in and he said, 'Similar boys."

Roy would go to the RSA after work from 5 pm-6 pm. He'd have a few beers and play some pool then he'd ring home and ask to be picked up. "We didn't have a licence but down we'd go in the Austin A40 and later the Hillman Super Mix and pick him up but as we got older, we'd do a few laps around the main street of town first."

Roy had a big garden and passed his skills on to his boys. Gardening was also encouraged by the primary school where each pupil was given a packet of seeds to take home, plant and look after. "Roy would clear a plot where I'd plant the seeds and later the teacher came around and graded how well you'd done," said Colin.

* * *

A Tale Told

"We had a heap of aunties and uncles that looked after us. We often volunteered to go with Uncle Bill to round up wild horses for the rodeo. I say volunteer but in hindsight, Bill had only a fat Corgi called Basil so he needed us boys because we were the closest to useful dogs he had. He'd take us out east in his old Ford Ute into the hill country. Hours later, he'd pull up at a gate down some narrow gravel road and us boys would climb out. Once you asked him, 'How big is this paddock, Uncle Bill?' He scratched his head under his cap and said, 'One thousand acres.' And you nodded not knowing how big a thousand acres was and shrugged and said, okay. Then he'd give us really basic instructions like, 'See that ridge line over there to the left, you boys climb up the top and walk along the fence until you get to the end then drop down into the bush.' And we'd all nod, yep, Uncle Bill we'll drop down into the bush. 'Then spread out. It's important to spread out and make a lot of noise as you come back towards me.'

And we'd smile like that was easy and off we'd go without any food or water. 'Don't drink out of the river,' he would warn. 'It's got poison in it due to poisoning the possums."

You quickly learnt the hills were high and a thousand acres was a lot and bush, tight with supplejack and clearings filled with blackberry were bloody hard work to get through. The horses were wild enough to fear a few boys hollering and screaming. Sometimes bushes would suddenly explode in front of you as mares, stallions and occasionally foals broke cover.

Late in the afternoon, your enthusiasm waned due to eight hours of work without food or water. You'd be carrying scratches and bruises, coughing dust and be scorched on the flats by the sun then you'd see Uncle Bill and the car miles away and suddenly your spirits would lift and you'd pick up your pace.

His appreciation came in the form of a reward when we got to the pub. Uncle Bill always stopped for a few beers and he'd bring us raspberry juice and packets of chips while we waited in the car. The first of these was a 1948 two-door coupé.

On the two occasions when Uncle Bill left the key in the ignition, your older brother Jim slid along to the driver's seat and told you to drop under the steering wheel to push in the clutch when he told you while your middle brother Rod changed gears. Off Jim would take us for a spin, but you saw nothing squeezed in between Jim's legs, the steering wheel and peddles. When Uncle Bill worked out what we were doing, he took the key with him but that didn't stop Jim from putting the car into gear and pulling the starter motor so we could still drive around the car park until the battery went flat. That was much better because you could look out the windows.

"Bloody kids," Uncle Bill would scold when he came out to find the battery was flat and he'd order us out to push. We'd be full of fizzy and chips and out we'd jump and push, bare feet skidding on the gravel as red-faced men in the pub stood at the windows and laughed.

"At school, we'd tell stories about our adventures getting the rodeo horses to encourage mates to replace the mates that wouldn't help again. When Uncle Bill upgraded to a Vanguard Ute, there'd be a tribe of us sitting on the tarpaulin covering the tray. As he sped out over gravel roads summer dust would cover us grey. When we finally jumped off outside some farm gate, it piled at our feet. After instructions we'd run off in clouds of dust, ghosting the hills to loop around behind the wild horses."

* * *

Children in rural towns and out in the country had a great deal of freedom. Often the only boundaries were the limits they put on themselves. "Once we watched two boys get swept away on rubber tubes in the flooded river behind our house," Colin told me. "We thought that looked fun so we went down to the local tyre shop and got inner tubes, blew them up, went back to the river and jumped in. Down the river, we'd be swept sometimes for two or three kilometres. We'd slow down when we got to a large pool and paddle to shore then run across paddocks, jump over fences and run back into town to do it again.

My older brother Rodney made a flying fox over a deep pool in the Patea River. The river was only about eight or nine metres wide. He tied number eight wire to a tree then we pulled it across the river and tied it to another tree on the opposite bank. With a pulley, he made from something he found in Roy's shed and a roller attached to a bit of wood we would hold onto it before jumping off the cliff top and flying across the river. You couldn't let go too early because there were rocks and you couldn't hold on too long otherwise you hit the bank on the other side. It was all about timing. No one ever got hurt. It was a lot of fun.

Growing up we had few restrictions. We were free to explore our limits but we knew how to behave around our elders. We had great respect for them, they taught us how to knuckle down and work hard, not to give up and the importance of family.

We always had family come around home for Christmas. Two shillings were always in the pudding. Whisky and gin, beer and laughter made for happy get-togethers. Five or six or seven aunties and uncles would turn up during the day. We swapped homes with Uncle Glen who lived in Waitara. We'd go fishing and white baiting in the river. Had a great time. I remember sitting on the footpath watching 'I Love Lucy' through the window at Walsh's Home Appliance Store. It was the first time we'd seen television.

Mum covered the areas Roy could not manage. She got me into New Zealand Forest Service as an apprentice diesel mechanic. I had to pass a School Certificate to get accepted. School streamed kids off that wanted to get a trade so we studied Technical Drawing, Woodwork and Engineering. They also had Trade Maths which was practical. I learnt to measure a circle, square, cylinder and an acre. It was easy when you could see the practical use of it.

Roy and Molly told us boys, 'If you want anything go out and earn it then you'll appreciate it more.'"

When children have the freedom to test their limits, it raises their self-awareness. They gain knowledge and skills from new experiences, learn to work in a team and look beyond boundaries to find solutions; they become more confident and outgoing and engage not just with people but with life in general.

* * *

Roger White
Tiverton, Devon

Image: Simeon Patience

Roger to Betty

> Peddle machine children
> make synthetic cut-outs
> for online twiddle-thumbs
> to match flip-flop fashion.

> Once three yards of cloth
> was the measure of a woman or a man,
> when needle and thread words
> tacked and pinned the pattern
> of my heart onto yours.

Roger was a third-generation draper. His grandfather Robert Henry White came to New Zealand at the age of nineteen with his cousin William in 1878. "It was a six-week steam and sails trip," Roger told me.

Robert had completed an apprenticeship in textiles gaining the skills and professional aptitude to work in big department stores such as Auckland's Smith and Caughey's. In 1893, he established his own store in Whanganui.

Robert found he had too much stock so in 1910 he sent his son, Donald to Stratford in Taranaki. He was surprised when Donald kept asking for more and more stock. This prompted him to sell up and head north. White's Drapers was part of Stratford for one hundred and sixteen years.

"The building was in two halves," said Roger. "Stables were behind for horse and dray and three shops faced the road out front. They offered ladies' and men's clothing, carpets and drapes, dresses, fabrics, wool, mattresses, flooring, curtains, blinds, millinery and household linens. At their busiest, Whites employed eighteen staff, all specialists in their trade."

Donald took over from his father in 1937 and Roger from him in 1979. Roger and his eighteen-year-old son Peter began working together in 1973. Together, they kept the business going as the retail world of textiles and fabrics began to change.

"I enjoyed working with father," said Roger. "He gave me knowledge about textiles and fabrics, about business and people but most importantly people. It's a fundamental truth, treat people like you would want to be treated and life and business will be just fine."

* * *

A Tale Told

You knew you were getting more clothes when Dad came home from town saying, "Got more dead and buried for you, son." And he'd throw you a parcel all knotted and tied with string.

The brown paper and smell of mothballs gave away the church shop so you knew what to expect. Mrs Pettigrew ran it and knew the comings and goings of the town, particularly the goings, telling her favourites when new boxes were about to arrive from the dearly departed.

I always felt awkward with me farm boy manners and spending more time working on the farm than in class. Dressed in dead men's clothes just made it worse. They made me feel stiff with guilt and fear and I've hated the smell of mothballs ever since.

* * *

Stuart Greenhill
Aberdeenshire and England

by Margie Copleston

My father drowned in a boating accident off the Taranaki coast. He was sixty-four years old. That was tragic on numerous levels but the most striking for me was the realisation I did not know him. He never spoke about his life, what his hopes and dreams had been, or what his childhood was like. The dead line until memory's last word and an unspoken man is unstitched of deed sprang from that realisation.

On a Beach

Time faded then was lost.
Sea claimed you it was filled with men.
Some were spent, but you had time to spend.
Time faded then was lost.

Unseeing 'til lost, you knew too late
things not said nor shared wouldn't wait,
pieces that made a stoic sea of men
all is memory after amen.

Cold wind came opened your mouth,
once spoke like lions' gulls flew out
beating soft till blue then nothing else.
Wind-like windows opened your mouth.

A flap of wave winged to shore too many
to count, too soft, one more.
Sea took you no choice you went
with that growl, that jug, time not spent

Time faded then was lost,
a granule too little too many too tossed
on a beach in a picture time faded then lost.

About the Poem

The omniscient voice is critical of the man who waits at sea to be rescued. He knows the man reflects on his life and realises after his funeral he exists only through memory. He also knows the man 'had time to spend', implying he dies before his time. That his death is 'soft' is conveyed by the image of a 'flap of wave' winging to shore. The image of a wave extends to the man as a granule of sand on a beach. There he will be lost and forgotten amongst all the other 'grains' because he has not 'said or shared' his life. The granule reinforces how quickly we will be lost and how insignificant we will become if not remembered.

The line 'in a picture time faded then lost' links nicely to earlier poems such as Taranaki Weka and The Old Man. In The Old Man, he sits in his chair looking at photographs on the wall and mantelpiece. He knows the story behind each photo, unlike the picture of the man's life in this poem. How many of us inherit a photograph album and have no idea what most of the pictures are about? Similarly, the old tunnel builders in Taranaki Weka look up at a photograph above the pool table knowing they will be 'seldom remembered.' The picture of the man as a granule of sand on a beach will fade. Its loss doubles the tragedy of his death.

* * *

My father and mother followed the 'accepted' way of bringing up their three sons.

- Haircuts were short back and sides. This was a hangover from the war which had ended fifteen years earlier.
- Circumcision was inflicted just in case another war broke out in a foreign desert somewhere at some future time.

- 'Torture clinics' were not questioned where dental nurses attacked healthy teeth to fill them with amalgam.
- Shorts were worn until you were thirteen.
- Suffering Sunday school was expected until you were old enough to run away on Sunday mornings.
- You were forced to eat everything on your plate, including broad beans while being lectured about the less fortunate in China and India.
- You learnt no dessert would come until you ate your mains including all the broad beans.
- Outdoor pursuits and participation in sports were unspoken expectations. It built healthy children. It was where you learnt to congratulate the winners and be humble in winning.

All the children around you had parents who did exactly the same, so you couldn't feel punished. When you grew older, it was natural to react against your parents which was the way to form a strong sense of identity and that of course led to independence.

During the difficult hormonal years of your teens, you realised your father was not 'perfect' or more realistically you recognised his faults which, of course, you expressed and were determined to avoid. How many of us think we have avoided them only to be told repeatedly we haven't?

Father's older brother inherited the family dairy farm when his father retired. Primogeniture dates to the Old Testament and surprisingly, it is still active today. Father trained as a Fat Stock Buyer, becoming an agent for Thomas Borthwick & Sons Limited. [38]. He studied through Massey University and knew all grades of wool just as he could estimate the weight of a sheep by sight.

Father was happy in his job. He enjoyed driving on narrow back country roads, gravel dust summers, and mud-wet winters. He respected the farmers, celebrated with them when prices were good and suffered along with them when they were low. You remember going drafting with him. You'd arrive at stockyards filled with hundreds of sheep. Father would collect the raddle from the cardboard box in the boot of his car, have a quick chat with the farmer then climb into the first pen and begin marking the lambs for the truck to pick up later in the day. Over time his back bent, his right shoulder muscled more than his left, his knees ached and his arms and neck burnt dark brown under constant sun. He would always stop in for a beer at the local pub before going home. There he'd talk to farmers about the schedule prices, rugby, cricket and politics. He'd bring his days home in the smell of sweat and wool on his clothes and sheep shit on his boots.

You hardly saw him in summer. Early mornings, he'd be up and gone and back home late, after a beer or two. If he wasn't on the road, he'd sit in his chair at night beside the phone ready to talk to his clients. No caller ID back in those days so he couldn't avoid any of the grumpy or boring ones. He always listened and informed and was respectful until he hung up.

Father arranged a load of split wood to be dropped at the back of the property every summer. You and your two older brothers would wheelbarrow and stack for months often overseen by father who checked the rows in the shed were stacked tight and uniform. He had a Presto-Rollmo. It was the motor mower equivalent of an untrained dog with its 98cc Villiers motor that sped up at corners, ignored adjustments to the throttle and tugged him along behind it. When you were old enough to use it, you realised the throttle was tricky. Out of the blue, it would lock onto full and take off forcing you to run after it and as you did, you'd be trying to disconnect the throttle while attempting to avoid Mother's primulas, hosts or any other low-growing border plants. Your older brother left it in the creek on one occasion.

We had a big vegetable garden. Father dug small trenches along a string line tied onto two bamboo stakes. Beans, broad beans (yuck), carrots, and peas were regimented in rows that rotated each season. Peas were our favourite because you could pick them straight off the plant and eat them raw. Us boys would raid neighbouring gardens just for their peas.

Vegetable gardening was part of our primary school education. Easy-to-grow vegetables that produced quickly were the hook for any child and radishes provided that. Nothing we grew went to waste. Mother froze, made chutney and with cases of cheap Hawkes Bay fruit made jams and preserves. We learnt to 'tickle' potatoes to get the new season's best, scratched ourselves on gooseberries and went blackberry picking as a family along gravel roads Father noted had plenty of roadside bushes.

Pre-Christmas, Father would often be given a lamb or two as a thank you from farmers. You'd watch and learn how to butcher it as it lay on a sheet on the kitchen table. It was probably the same way he had learnt. Carving a chook was similar but to cull, gut and pluck one was like a massacre when Father was involved. It began when he stood at the chopping block on the lawn outside the chook pen. Axe in one hand and an egg-bound chook hanging upside down from the other he'd begin. There was a passive dignity to Red Shavers as they surrendered to the guillotine. After each head was chopped off, Father would let them run claiming 'The little buggers bleed out quicker.' Mother saw it very differently when, on occasions a chook's desperation to find its head had it running under the freshly washed sheets on the clothesline. You only remember Father ever plucking and gutting one chook as a demonstration; then it was left to us three boys to do the rest.

Mother did all the cooking but father was there when any meat or fish needed slicing. Sharpening the carving knife with the steel was one of his rituals, a show of his skill. "Feel that, boy," he'd say, after a few switches, switch, switches of the knife against the steel. And you would touch the knife edge with your finger. "Careful! I could shave with it." The knife and steel had bone handles and the maker's touchmark Sheffield stamped on them. They were inherited from Mother's father whose family had brought them out from Aberdeenshire. You'd watch father hold the roast or chicken in place with the fork while he thinly sliced the meat with the knife. He had the talent to make meat go a little further, particularly when he had three growing boys to feed but we had plenty of vegetables. Harvesting what we could from the garden, sea and land was part of a generation that just got off their backsides and did it.

Health stamps that came out in the 1970s captured most families in New Zealand. Sport was a large part of growing up. Father never missed taking his boys down to athletics on a Tuesday evening. All the 'health stamp' boys and girls met to sprint or run around Victoria Park. Fathers and mothers would line up at the finish line with different coloured batons to give first, second and third. Creosote lines marked the track, chimney smoke hung low on winter evenings along with the cigarette smoke from parents cheering on from the grandstand. Although place winners were acknowledged it really wasn't about that when you were six, nine, eleven. It was about your body, the way it moved, the sprint you could get out of it, the panting joy at the end of the race when you were told you'd run a good race regardless of your place, and the big men, the older boys all seeing you as they had once been seen. As your body grew stronger, it came with a strong sense of who you were and what you could do.

Father never hit us, initially, we got a smack on the bum but after that, it was all verbal. With a smack, the sting fades quickly but verbal assaults linger forever. There was a litany of put-downs in the mouths of men at the time: you could look 'gormless', 'be soft as butter', which meant you were 'weak as water', and if you cried then you cried like a 'motherless foal' and looked like a 'chinless wonder'. Those were the phrases that attempted to straighten you out, 'knock you down a peg or two' in the same way as being strapped at primary school, caned at high school, or you were held back if you didn't pass School Certificate or University Entrance. As old soldiers faded out of politics and learning institutions, corporal punishment faded out with them leaving 'useless bastards' like me to sit in stuffy classrooms writing outlines with other useless bastards after school.

Echoing in my head now are those men, including Father telling me hardship and knockbacks 'build backbone' and fortitude and perseverance. They attempted to turn you into a Supertramp song that insisted you should be sensible, responsible, practical and dependable at the expense of what? A 'good' man needs all those, a complete man needs the balance of art and for that, you need a place to contemplate, the archetypal cave or a fire to sit beside or an art gallery, bookshop or music shop, yes, places like those.

Mother said father had my best interests at heart when he attempted to get me into farming but when that didn't work, he arranged a tour through the Wairata freezing works. He hoped I would take up the opportunity to train as a manager. This meant beginning on the ground floor, working in each department over a period of three years before advancing into management.

Father's friend Mr Jennings led the way, beginning where beef was slaughtered. Gruesome enough but when we moved through to the chain where highly skilled butchers, pulled pelts off, gutted and boned the carcasses, any belief that father and the manager would protect you evaporated. What began as a slow rhythmical bang, bang, bang of knife handles on stainless steel tables built to a crescendo accompanied by a deep drone of 'Who's that bastard? Who's that bastard? Who's that bastard?' You looked up at Mr Jennings who looked shocked and terrified as he quickly ushered us up metal steps to the exit on the first floor.

Father never insisted on me taking that job. I was quite happy to accept his assessment that I was too soft to survive in that environment but I did appreciate that he wanted to keep me alive.

Previous generations had little choice but to stay on the farm, daughters tended to marry farmer's sons, and farmer's sons tended to marry farmer's daughters. Now farmer's daughters run farms and more and more sons have left for the cities. Some parents who want to retire can't leave the farm because their children don't want to work it. Prices are too high for the properties to sell so fences tilt, gates unhinge, bracken and blackberry, manuka, dock and ragwort have the freedom to spread. Today many farms are leased or managed which supports Collie Hancock's statement that each generation makes the next generation's lives a little easier. Freedom to choose our futures comes from the toil and sacrifice of preceding generations but that shouldn't be at the cost of their values.

Father died at sea which might sound heroic and adventurous but in fact, it was not. It denied me a 'last-words peaceful out of breath death,' Roger McGough so aptly described in his poem 'Let Me Die a Young Man's Death.' If the emotional side of our relationship had been satisfied, then if father went out in a 'hail of bullets' or was 'shot by gangsters' and even drowned at sea it would not have left me feeling cheated. In my eulogy, I stated how important it was for fathers to talk to their sons because the dead live until memory's last word, and an unspoken person is unstitched of deed.

We can't shed the painful moments of our youth, why would we want to? Those moments formed us and left lingering memories most of us would have learnt from. Injustice, cruelty and hurt, winning and losing are part of life. Sheltering children from those realities denies them the strength to address their own shortcomings or to deal with the flaws in others.

* * *

Puppies in Sacks

From Stuart's novel, Dante Fog.
Austin & McCauley Publishers Ltd.

You had watched Grandfather roll back to the shed on his buggered hips and hook the whimpering litter out from under it with his crook and drop them into a sack with a rock.

When you heard the tractor start, you raced outside to watch Grandmother bounce on the seat of the Massey Ferguson as she drove down the hill to the river. Grandfather bum-hopped on the tray at the back, and you could hear him humming hymns because he couldn't pout to whistle on account of his stroke. You ran to the corner of the garden and snuck through the hole in the hedge and watched as the tractor puttered beside the river and then, with his strong right arm, Grandfather heaved the sack into the water.

You imagined it slowly sinking, the blind puppies pawing each other as the cold water rushed over their naked bodies, and the light sealed to black as they softly butted the scrim and drowned.

When you told your father what had happened, he dismissed your childish response with a reality check about farming. "Better to have been drowned than knocked on the head with a hammer," he replied. It was short and succinct, practical and honest but you thought he missed the point.

* * *

Ben

A farmer had given father a puppy that we called Ben. Mother was not impressed when she saw how big his paws were. "He's going to ruin my garden with those big feet," she warned. Ben had a shaggy brown coat and a healthy bark. Father said the bark was because he came from good huntaway stock though the rest of us thought the dog was given to Father because he was the runt of the litter and would be useless. When you asked why the farmer gave him the dog, Father replied, as he usually did when the question was difficult, "Don't be so stupid."

You quickly learnt that Ben not only barked but also stole clothing from the neighbourhood clotheslines and he nipped. Nipping was tolerated and kind of cool when he was only two or three months old but as he grew so did the need for your stride to lengthen. He had an instinct to herd and would wait at the gate for you after primary school to put it into practice, nipping and barking at your heels as you raced up the long drive to the house.

You knew Ben's days were numbered living in town with those huntaway skills. Mother had told Father it was just a matter of time for 'that dog to get himself into trouble.' That day arrived when I came home late from school. To my relief, Ben was not waiting at the gate, which allowed me to check the letterbox for mail without being assaulted. At I checked, I heard children yelling 'help!' and crying.

Next door lived the Pickering's. The driveway into their garage had high concrete walls on either side which were impossible to climb. When I walked up the street to see where all the noise was coming from, I found Ben had bailed half a dozen frightened and crying children against the Pickering's' garage door. Thankfully, the Pickering's were not at home. I snuck up behind Ben, grabbed him by his collar and pulled him away allowing the children to scatter. "You've done it now, boy," I told him.

Sure enough, Father received phone calls that evening complaining about Ben. His apology was overlaid with bewilderment that 'these people' could not *see the natural talent of the dog. After we had matched the six names with the six children Ben had penned, Father relaxed in his chair and looked at you. "The farmer gave me that dog boy because he knew how bloody good, he was. He'll be worth a pretty penny when properly trained mark my words." Father's pride was dented but he gained a win of sorts until the following morning when you saw him drop Ben into the boot of the car. The dog seemed totally unaware of his circumstance as all his focus was on one of Mother's slippers he held in his mouth. He sat challenging you or anyone to have a go at getting the slipper back. Father winked, "Don't tell your mother. I'm in enough trouble as it is." You nodded, happy to share a secret. We were all relieved to see the dog go, last seen crouching with a snarl as the boot lid dropped over him.*

* * *

Illustration: Murry Hill

Lighting Fires

Father boasted he knew how to keep the home fire burning. Lucky for him, Mother was happy to close three-quarters of the house in winter to keep us all warm, giving the kitchen fire a credibility it would have otherwise lacked. On 21 April, the door down the passage was shut; the door from the kitchenette to the main lounge was shut as was the door to the laundry and bathroom. The kitchenette was open plan, divided between the kitchen and a small living area. Father and Mother's chairs sat on each side of the fireplace, in front of them was the kitchen table squeezed between the television and front window.

Although our house had two fireplaces the one in the lounge was rarely used. According to Father, it was an example of 'piss-poor' workmanship because all the heat went up the chimney and all the smoke billowed back into the room.

During summer, trailer loads of wood were dumped on the back lawn for you three boys to wheelbarrow and stack in the shed. Father was always there to inspect each load. He knew the right wood to buy. It had to be hand-split Macrocarpa or Pinus Radiata. He was part of a generation that doubted the contribution modern machinery gave to firewood. Honest manual toil always took precedence over wood that had been 'buggered around by machines.'

Each year, Father set down the first row of wood for the stack then disappeared and left you to it. Neatness was everything. Bringing the wood to the shed was a discipline and a necessity. It was hard work particularly when you were five and it slowly morphed as you grew older into a tedious weekend chore.

Father taught you how to set a fire just in case he came home late or was ill and couldn't. It was unsaid but you knew it was a handy skill if you got lost in the jungle or wanted to cook a wild pig or deer or ended up in a winter war zone in Europe; yes, Europe after being prepared for a desert in summer. Pyramids were the most efficient design, not too much paper and not screwed too tightly, otherwise, well it smouldered rather than spread evenly under the kindling.

Father knew the size of the kindling that ignited quickly but did not burn too fast, giving larger pieces of wood a chance to catch. He knew cutting kindling required a skillset that developed with time. It began with selecting the right piece of wood. It should be without knots and bark because the bark will fall off and make a mess in the wood cupboard and bark often harboured moisture or slaters or both. Mother hated slaters. She scalded them dead with hot water from the jug but for Father moisture was the enemy.

He knew how to give a smouldering fire an oomph by holding a sheet of newspaper across the hearth to draw air under the grill. That's if the paper didn't catch fire from the small brown expanding dot in the middle. And he knew when and what size wood to add and when the fire was ripe for coal. It was like a Chinese tea ceremony in our house and only occurred between television adverts. This allowed Father time to climb out of his chair and fill the hearth shovel from the copper coal scuttle with just the right amount of coal and gently disperse it across the fire as he muttered a mantra of curses against mining companies and government levies. Coal was expensive so he used it sparingly unless he was particularly pleased about a rugby result or had been to the pub which often meant the door down the passage could be opened. When you watched Father stretch his legs beside the fire or sit back in his chair with his hands behind his head, he seemed content and happy, almost smug like he knew he had succeeded in providing comfort and warmth for his family.

The coal man's deliveries depended on Father's moods. You watched from the kitchen window as he backed his old Ford truck up the drive and stopped outside the garage beneath the house. Coalman then walked to the back of his truck, lined himself up with a sack and pulled it down onto his back. He was short and hairy and always covered in black dust, wore a leather apron over a black singlet in winter and was bent like all the weight from the sacks had buckled his back.

Your older brother told your father that fires were not good for the environment.

"Rather freeze, would you?" Father always exaggerated when he was defensive.

"All the smoke and deforestation aren't good." His class had done a project on pollution, so he knew his stuff.

"What would you have me do?" Father asked. "Jam a whopping big filter down the chimney?"

"That wouldn't stop trees being cut down or mining, would it?" That tag question he used really pissed Father off. You'd see his jaw clench and his mouth tighten before something really stupid came out.

"This is what happens when all those left-wing airy-fairy, dreadlock and drug-induced mumbo-jumbo teachers brainwash the kids," he'd say to Mother. "They turn them into stupid bloody know-alls."

Father could pick sparks off the mat with his fingers and flick them back into the fire, he could light his cigarette between the bars of the grill without getting burnt. He would stoke the fire with coal before bed and in the morning if he was lucky, restart it with the embers left in the grate. Or he might find a gem of coal glowing in the ash bucket as he took it outside to empty. Pinched between two sticks of kindling he would come running back inside with much noise and urgency, calling,

"Watch out! Watch out! Out of my way! It's still alive!" and dash through the house to the fireplace with the glowing fragment of coal hoping to make the day special. Kneeling in front of the fireplace, he'd place small dry shavings of wood over the ember and blow gently. It might take a few minutes or thirty to get a flame; then he'd stand and exclaim, "There!" and point down at the wee flickering flame. "Perseverance, boys, is all it takes." And your older brother would say, "Well done, Father, you've saved a match but it's not a tree, is it?"

The fire warmed our legs, buttocks, hands and our pyjamas. It dried clothes and sports boots. It was a communal area where aunties sat and nattered, where lead-head nails were melted for sinkers. When the power went out or on Sunday evenings, toasties were made in the quicksie machine Mother got from McKenzie's. Potatoes were roasted inside their jackets, chestnuts exploded amongst the coals sending embers onto the mat to the scowling disapproval of Father who hated his fire in disarray.

Every time the town's fire siren went, Mother would ask if the chimney needed cleaning provoking Father to scold, "Of course not." He always waited to see whether the fire engine passed the front window to some 'silly bastard's house' down the street.

You were reminded of lanky 'Chim chimney, chim chimney' sweeps each autumn when Father pulled the chimney sweep from off the shed roof. He had made it from two old rake handles nailed and wired together and the head of a garden hoe bolted on the end. This flimsy construction was handed up to us boys as we stood on the roof by the chimney. You had to wait for the 'all clear' from

Mother before you could start. She covered the carpet and lino in the kitchenette with newspaper and old sheets ready to collect the detritus. Her plan wasn't always successful when slabs of soot dropped in large chunks and exploded in the grate sending clouds of ash into the kitchen. You always knew when that happened because her shrieks echoed up through the chimney as she raced about waving a tea towel trying to contain the ash.

After scraping the inside of the chimney from the roof, you attacked it from below with a wire brush. Our fireplace was tiny compared with the 'Banks' fireplace but that didn't stop at least one attempt by each of us boys to see how far you could climb inside before you got stuck and someone had to pull your legs to get you back out.

Every summer, Father tested the patience of entire streets depending on the direction of the wind when he stoked green garden waste and hedge clippings into billowing clouds of smoke. For days, it would drift across rooftops and fences, hedges and roads searching for washing on clotheslines. On one occasion, an angry neighbour called the fire brigade. An engine arrived outside our house with its siren blaring and lights flashing. Firemen dropped out of the cab grabbing hoses and running up the drive dragging them behind. Around the side of the house to the back of the property they went, flattening Mother's border plants and ring barking trees. They found Father standing beside his fire, probably musing over the silly bastard who needed the brigade and totally oblivious to the fact he had cancelled half the sky with smoke…or was he?

* * *

Father retired early due to brucellosis and arthritis. He found that extremely difficult though he never shared how much losing his job meant. He stopped going to his local where many of his farming clients drank and became a regular at another pub. There he found solace amongst retired farmers where he drank his jug, smoked without the fear of being caught (supposedly he had given up decades ago) played pool and sometimes helped behind the bar.

I respected his commitment to the family, his boys' sport, and the community. He was a member of the Lions and Swimming Clubs, a board member at the local high school and ran the school farm. I didn't learn carpentry or engineering or plumbing or electrical skills from him but I have applied on numerous occasions, his ability to Frankenstein a 'tool' from bits and pieces to get a job done.

Morrison

Voices from the past echo down through tales. Often these are embellished by licence of 'Chinese whispers but the essence of the story holds true. Harrowing events such as the tale of Morrison still reverberate in the community. There is a certain gallantry about Morrison after his youth was sacrificed during the First World War and later at his own hands.

Mr Morrison returned from war having fought in Gallipoli and France. He was a man who, having paid his dues returned to New Zealand with the hope of owning a farm. The chance came when he won a ballot for an undeveloped block of land in an isolated area of hill country in Taranaki. What happened to Morrison is a cautionary tale about governments, war, banks, debt and love

Morrison's story reflects the qualities respected and admired at the time. Robert Bly stated, 'We are all forged by life's trials and tribulations but not all of these must be personal. We can gain valuable lessons from those we are told or witnessed.' [2]

* * *

He watched the devil whip the darkness with fire that devoured his house. Silhouetted by the blaze he cast a long shadow across the frosted paddock behind him. An inferno raged inside his heart, it was stronger than the eastern sun rising behind the mountains, tiripapā manawa, tiripapā kōrua he heard the hills rumble around him, exploding heart, exploding pit, Gallipoli was in his head.

The valley amplified the dawn chorus of Magpie, Korimako and Tui. Morrison knew it would voice the approach of any vehicle from five miles out. His cold eyes turned past the flames down the drive to the bridge and gravel road beyond and thought of another parameter breach. He must move now. Sunrise in the east where the Aegean Sea should have been, house ablaze to the west and in between the carcasses of his dead stock. They lay strewn across the paddock from an order he carried in his head, 'Leave nothing for the enemy. Burn, blowup or shoot anything you cannot carry.' Morrison cradled his rifle and walked across the paddock to set the sheds alight.

Conscripted some men died, the rest came home,
the rest came home, some died.
They returned, swinging arms marching
behind bagpipes kilted pleats,
once suns now filled with holes
and wounds and limping minds
as children ran beside them dreaming of a day
when they too would march to the same drum beat
and pipes.

He had survived Gallipoli and Armentieres. Shrapnel in his legs had brought him home,

to skies filled with bunting and cheer,
where he drank to keep his pride and screamed
to bandage nightmares that oozed orange
then dried to bruise.
And he swallowed his words for sanity's sake
knowing bodies in no man's land were made of them.

In nineteen hundred and nineteen, he won a ballot for two hundred acres of scrub and bush in the eastern blocks of Taranaki. A repatriation loan from the government bought him a horse and gear and a dog he called Colin.

Zeitoun. We lost our virginity there, remember?
At the Wazza.
Yeah, you were so fucking quick, you thought you could have two women for the price of one.
I was blonde, they should have paid me!
After your performance? Not likely.
Drunken nights singing then full kit marching with sand, flies and that blistered fucking sun.

We were young and uncaged.
Remember the Zoological gardens where you first got the itch and the houseboats along the banks of the Nile?
We were going to go back after the war and buy one.

Morrison headed east where large swathes of country had been cleared. Stumps still smouldered and burned. He remembered the tree-covered hills before he was conscripted. They had risen like youth's free will on a flap of a wing towards the sun, now they lay like bodies on a battlefield.

One hundred and fifty acres he cleared that first year. How quickly he had stripped the hills with axe and burnt them to ash leaving bones of pigs tangled in supplejack and kiwi burnt in burrows. He tore the throat from the voice box of nature until the land became silent and sullen and empty. He set the wind free to speak the dust of pharaohs and eastern emperors, of bullets pierced and mud brute marches, of mates killed, tears wept, the vibration of bombs, of terrified voices, last words spoken and youths' broken wings.

He wanted silence. He wanted boundaries. He wanted perimeters and vistas to defend. He split logs into posts and dug them deep then stapled barbed wire to battens that caught only wool from his Romney sheep.

Everything was thriving in the twenties. He built a small house on the rise. The bloke in the next block could not make a go of it so he borrowed and bought it, extending his farm to six hundred acres. Then he shot his foot in 1923.

Don't remember that.
Well, you were there.
Where?
Hunting up the valley behind the house.
No, I wasn't.
I always took my gun on account of the pigs.
Plenty of blokes were charged for not carrying their weapons.
As I said, I was hunting and climbed between the wires of a fence but got distracted by my dog, Colin.
What?
Colin, my dog.
Why'd you name him that?
After you.

What do you mean, after?
So, anyway I got hooked on the barbed wire and the gun went off.
You had a bullet in the breech! That was stupid.
Yep. Bullet went right through the side of my right foot.
Idiot!
Held it together with strips I tore off my shirt.
Disability was a matter of perspective after the war. He cleared another one hundred and thirty acres after the accident.

I wouldn't have met Margarete if I hadn't damaged my foot. She did tell me no man is worth marrying if he couldn't dance. She was French.

Morrison thought marriage wasn't for him anyway. Along with mistrusting politicians, lawyers, and accountants, he had no time for religion, so they lived quite happily in other people's 'sins.

Margarete had come to New Zealand looking for peace and quiet. The most isolated vacancy for a district health nurse she could find was at Tahora, one hundred and eighteen kilometres from the city. Despite the remoteness, she could not escape the noise of war.

They were a perfect match. She was three years older, full-figured, with a slight stoop as if the war had removed some of her bones. Her voice was raspy like sand had lined it when she nursed in the desert. Only nicotine and strong drinks stopped all her memories of the dead from climbing back out, that was what she told people. Her hair was short with strands of grey and the large dark pupils of her eyes seemed permanently fixed on seeing in the dark.

Evenings on the porch, they sat and drank and smoked and tried not to talk about the past. Long silences filled with the comfort of knowing each other was there. He rolled his flake-cut tobacco into perfect cigarettes but when his hands shook too much Margarette made them. "If bullets, illness, gas and shrapnel didn't kill you," he told her, "Government gave you tobacco."

Then came the Depression, then letters from the bailiff with his derby hat and pinched black suit. The wireless told them the government had bought land at inflated prices. Mortgages and costs were high while returns were continually dropping. When wool was at three pence a pound one year, the next no value at all he felt the hills closing in.

They left to fight, some died, the rest came home, the rest came home, some died.

No one blamed her for leaving, they said. *'It must have been hard living with a man like that, with his foot and wounds and evenings spent drinking.'*

'She had done her time overseas, poor dear. It was time to put herself first for a change.'

'A fair honest woman, foreign mind, but on the right side. He'll be lost without her. Lost.'

But he had insisted she leave. Told her he would follow in time. Midday, he hitched the horse to the dray to take her to the train station. Two suitcases bounced under canvas on the deck as the wheels rolled through mud ruts and potholes. His oilskin covered her legs to keep her dress and polished shoes clean. His voice was low encouraging the horse; 'That a boy,' 'Steady,' 'On yah go' that he had bought at a clearing sale. His name was 'Mo'. He had one eye.

Margarette sat silent and rigid under her brolly. Her tight pout accentuated her cheekbones coloured rouge in the face of the cold wind. He slumped inside his shoulders. Withdrew behind his beard. He raged inside shafts of rain that raced down the valley towards them. Splinters of light steeled the sky then beat the hills with thunder. Clouds torn from the sky, filled with rain hang over the valley and hills. He bent to the chilled sou-wester. His knuckles tight to the rain as all around everything jumped high to grey dissolving paddocks, the track, the fence line, and he welcomed the torrent. When he looked across at Margarette, she had closed her brolly and surrendered to it. Her hand clasped his as she slid closer. The horse plodded with his head down. The cloak of rain held them inside a world that was briefly theirs.

The locomotive gave an impatient hiss as Margarete glanced back one last time before stepping into the carriage. It belched black smoke as steel upon steel heaved the train from the platform. The station guard limped back to his room past Morrison, "Not for long I hope," he muttered. Morrison shrugged. Left standing beneath the station clock, he felt a bayonet stuck in the trench of his heart, tick-tock, tick-tock. Ash-to-ash fell onto the platform as he clutched her tears in his handkerchief. He watched sheep on the flats surge away from the iron monster he knew too well. It threw the mob to the corners of paddocks, swept them back in retreat then turned them around to charge again back over the dead at their feet. And every edge broke to his whistle, to her voice, to fragmented colour, to snatch a bark from dust-dry air to the Muybridge gallop of horse in the air, a dash of legs across no man's land when he sang guitar with Colin on the troop-train, fox-trotted on talcum with Khepri in Cairo, and sipped Stella beneath Bougainvillea near Wassir.

Little Tommy Sangster arrived at the house a week later. He had split his legs to straddle the publican's draft horse and rode twenty plodding miles to warn Morrison, 'Bailiff at the pub. Says he's coming here tomorrow morning.' Morrison fed Tommy cold meat and chutney and gave him a sack filled with Margarete's preserves then sent him on his way.

He smoked the last of his tobacco as shells exploded all around. "Retreat," the sergeant hollered. "Retreat! Leave nothing for the enemy. Retreat predawn and be gone."

Morrison set the house and sheds ablaze and shot his stock as he heard the scarred hills cry, "Get the medic!" He tucked the rifle beneath his arm and limped to the dugout he'd made up-hill sixty. It was a place in Gallipoli where the sun was caged where he heard and watched through a hole in his head the essence of being human and dead.

It was years later that a pig hunter's dog found the hole Morrison had dug into the papa bank. His bones were collected and brought back for burial. The community turned out to show their respect, Margarette never returned.

They left to fight, some died, the rest came home, the rest came home. [39]

* * *

Loss, love, hardship, sacrifice, ambition, despair and betrayal are part of the human condition. The tragedy of Morrison plays out like a Shakespearean play and its importance is reflected in the number of times it was told to me.

If you watch the Olympics to celebrate individual endeavours rather than a waving flag, then you might see the possibility of the world being bordered not by tribal boundaries but by the human condition. Without them, we can praise our strengths and support our weaknesses because quite frankly, we are just groups of people living in different areas of the planet. Extending that thought to families, sure there are cultural differences but the overall desire of a parent for a child is basically the same worldwide. Human tragedies such as Morrison's have universal appeal because the circumstances and suffering are recognisable. Remember the man who saved the ewe in the flooded river? Neither drowned right, but that story is told and retold like Morrison's because it reflects qualities of being human that are admirable.

* * *

Great-Uncle Glen was one of several uncles who fought in the First World War. At eight or nine years of age, those men seemed large, taciturn and intolerant of children. I suppose all adults would have appeared large at that age but the other descriptions seem accurate enough. However, that probably had less to do with them returning from war and more a reflection of the social hierarchy. At that time, children were meant to be seen and not heard, earned their advancement and recognition with study and hard work and that of course came with age.

* * *

Great-Uncle Glen

Us kids laughed when we saw his wooden leg
told in whispers war took his femur
which sounded less painful than a tooth
when loss was tragic for a day
when pain was magnified by youth.
Hugger off, your ids!

Another bullet went through his left ear
came out through his jaw
he chewed his words with half a tongue
which made us giggle even more.
Hugger off, your ids!

We laughed not knowing war ignited nerves
across his face. Flares over no-mans-land
where men advanced, less retreated as he lay
in his mud bed thinking he was dead.

Now war is a seriousness talked into a face like
refugees in the Mediterranean, war in the Ukraine or
Palestine or, someone losing a cat.
It is bunting and a bugle on Anzac Day, a restless silence,
a boulder crocheted onto a chair, stained with dribbles
and mashed food. War is a delusion like saying
the dead are resting or saying they'd been lucky,
lucky 'god' brought them home.

You studied his grey bulk rugged and slippered wondering
how nurses would ever remove him.
How do you remove a battlefield after you have seen it?
How do you unsee what has never been said?
And laughter magnified by youth, hijacked by glimpses,
occasional visits and incomprehensible knowing,
collapsed into piteous tears, loud futile tears

Great Uncle Glen

About the Poem

'Great-Uncle Glen' is based upon a true story. He was a private in the First World War. Fighting in France, he was shot during an advance at the battle of Ypres. The bullet went through his left ear and came out through his right jaw. It left him lying unconscious in the mud as the allies advanced and then retreated. As they withdrew over the dead and dying, a young sherpa discovered Private Glen was still alive and carried him back to the aid station.

As children, we were too young to truly understand what happened to Great Uncle Glen. We were scolded when we laughed at his lisp and limp, and when we asked what happened to him, the reply was censored. Laughing highlighted our ignorance and disguised our fear. When we were old enough to understand what had happened, he was living in a rest home.

The contrast between him stained with dribbles and mashed food and the pomp and ceremony of Anzac Day is irreconcilable. Men who returned from the war made significant impressions on the following generations who remembered them not as characters in a book, poem or movie but in real life, and that taught them what sacrifice truly meant. Euphemisms, 'the dead were resting' and those that returned were 'lucky god brought them home' highlights the foolish glorification of war. Remember Rupert Brooke's veneration of a soldier's death, how it could transform 'some corner of a foreign field' into a piece of England?

Understanding what his uncle had been through is summarised in the final stanza where his tears are piteous and futile. They are 'futile' because he cannot change what his uncle had been through, and 'piteous' because his 'knowing' is insignificant.

* * *

Some ex-service people would not allow rifles onto their properties or go to Anzac Parades, some drank excessively and carried physical and psychological injuries for the rest of their lives, while others were lucky to return with a magnified view of the preciousness of life and lived to its fullest. Regardless of their approach to life, the war's impact rippled down through their families.

* * *

Monte Casino Archie

Monte Casino Archie was the name people called my dad. Me and Mum lived with his post-traumatic stress disorder behind his garage and petrol station on the main road. Archie was an engineer during the war. He knew how to construct and deconstruct things pretty much like he did with his face. He carried a puggy scarlet grimace he called a smile that hung with disappointed rage. He carried his post-traumatic stress disorder as a dodge, duck, sidestep and scuttle as he walked across the forecourt of the petrol station. He named his dogs Krout and Wop as cringing reminders of the five brutal years he spent at the war.

At seven years old, I was allowed to help on the forecourt. Archie had everything strictly controlled right down to his spit-polished boots that I cleaned each evening. Mum did all the accounts and worked the till, while I swept and filled and cleaned after school and at the weekends.

As we were on the main road, bikie gangs regularly stopped to fill up. You'd hear them coming miles away and stand out on the road and watch their advance. Like small black flies, they'd rumble closer and closer prompting Archie to call out, 'Here they come. Everyone into your positions.' Everyone being Mum and me.

Mum stopped whatever she was doing and manned the till as I stood in front of it waiting for Archie's pep talk and instructions. He'd count us off, 'one, two' then hand me the red fire extinguisher and remind Mum about the bat. 'Remember Dorothy, if there's trouble!' Mum just shook her head in disbelief. She had arthritis in her right shoulder and elbow and had no chance of wheeling the cricket bat to defend the till or herself. Archie had high expectations of his unit. 'We can do this. We're a small unit but we have not been beaten yet.' This always motivated me to do my duty the best I could as I stood holding the fire extinguisher. He would drop a cigarette lighter into the top pocket of his shirt before he and I marched out to the two bowsers.

You'd hear a thundering racket of bikes as they approached revving and changing down gears. 'Here come the bastards!' Archie would yell, challenging the noise and the prospect of being outnumbered by the enemy. As they rolled up to each browser he'd yell, 'Line up, you bastards. Line up! One at a time,' his arms and hands waving madly.

It never got less terrifying; me standing there with the fire extinguisher as these huge men rolled in. I recall one bikie rolled up to a bowser wearing a Nazi helmet and had a Swastika stitched on the sleeve of his jacket. Archie stood staring at him before walking over and leaning really close to the man's face. "I killed men that wore shit like this," he snarled, finger jabbing at the Swastika, at the helmet, his red hair flaming, face scarlet, brow knotted, eyes tightly locked onto the face of the bikie. The bikie-man had nothing, dropped his head and rode away.

After that first time, I asked Archie why he had the lighter. He winked and pulled it from his pocket, tossed it in the air and caught it again. 'Any trouble, boy, I'd douse them with petrol, toss the fuck'n lighter and run.' I remember laughing thinking he was joking but he just stared back in silence, so I stopped, nodded and muttered, "Good plan, Archie."

"That's why you've got the extinguisher, son. Just in case I catch on fire."

I was a little frightened of him but really glad he was on our side.

* * *

The longline

Taking the liberty of myth-making and a little hyperbole, the following memory is of a son paddling a longline of baited fishhooks out to sea. The first challenge for the boy was to get over the breakers before paddling one kilometre and dropping a sandbag anchor attached to the line. His older brothers pushed him through the churning white water until it became too dangerous, forcing them to return to the beach.

From Dante Fog by Stuart Greenhill.
Austin Macauley Publishers Ltd.

Between your legs, you saw the wet sand sinker and behind all of Father's hopes and dreams; sixty, eighty, one hundred hooks. And the paddle was a seven-foot-long piece of doweling with a piece of plywood screwed into it at each end and it was tied onto the front of the skiff so if you fell off you didn't lose the paddle. Bailing twine circled the tapered front so you could hook your feet under it. It would stop you from falling off, which happened. Punched off by a foaming fist. Lifted off and back onto the hooks. That thought gave you the shits...In front of you was the open ocean and you'd paddle pulling out line and you'd feel excited, then you wouldn't, then you would. And as you paddled, you'd turn back hoping you saw the waving towel signalling to drop the sinker and return. Five minutes. Ten. Out you paddled. And everyone on the beach got smaller— the beach, the cliffs, father. Twenty minutes, everything getting smaller. Seagulls squawked over the paddle that dipped and dripped and the skiff that bumped across a rippled blanket of water as you headed for Australia.

After you dropped the bag, you knew Father would be walking in angry circles on the beach. "What's that boy doing? He's dropped the bloody thing!" And his arms would fly up in the air with exasperation and he'd wave furiously at the reel. "Look there's still line on the bloody reel! He could have gone out further than that! No one signalled! Did anyone signal?" And he'd turn to whichever of his sons was on the beach and they'd shake their head. "No. No one signalled." And then he'd stomp down to the water's edge and stare out at the ocean with his hands in his pockets and mutter, "He could have gone a lot further. I could have thrown it bloody further! Weak as bloody water."

* * *

It seems sons are programmed, despite continual put-downs and perceived disappointments to please their fathers. I know some fathers told their mates at the racing club or at the pub just how proud they were of their sons. It wasn't something they told their boys because everything else, but words did. I wonder how many of us still feel driven to prove to the ghosts of our fathers, our worth.

* * *

A Handful of Dust

I was reminded repeatedly during this project of an incident in Evelyn Waugh's novel A Handful of Dust when six-year-old John Andrew Last was killed while riding his horse. The incident came quite unexpectedly like all tragedies but unlike Frederick William Meyers' family, it was fictional. What happened to Meyers is a fitting end to the book because I could not conclude it without mentioning the hardships endured and sacrifices made by women during this period and of course the influence they had on their children.

Fredrick was born in Auckland in 1864 and married Sarah Coulton in 1889. She had immigrated from Queen's County, Ireland in 1886. Frederick was described as a Farm Labourer on their marriage certificate.

New Zealand was a depressed state during the last decades of the nineteenth century. With little work available in Auckland, Frederick left for Taranaki to find employment in sawmills and building roads. Sarah later followed, after giving birth to their second daughter. She travelled by boat in open seas with a newborn in her arms and a toddler at her side.

The Seddon Government decided to stimulate the economy and get men working by establishing in 1893 the 'Improved Farm Settlement Blocks'. The scheme was aimed at getting the unemployed, mostly in the cities to work the land. These blocks were also open to ballot for men working on the roads. As part of the Government 'deal', men who won ballots would have to spend part of their week building or maintaining the roads.

Frederick won a ballot and immediately set about clearing his farm of bush. He built a basic house and established ten dairy cows which he milked by hand. Cans of milk were transported each day by horse and cart to the factory. When his daughters Annie and Ethel were old enough, they did this chore. The girls worked hard helping their father milk morning and evening and clear the land. Frederick and Sarah had another child they named Bill.

Frederick carried out his obligation to work on the roads labouring eight hours a day for eight shillings a week. One morning, he left home and never returned. Explosives were used by the men to blast down banks and open cuttings. On this day, a bag of blasting powder ignited critically burning him. Other road labourers wrapped him in their clothes before he was carried in a wagon two kilometres to the nearest town which was Strathmore. Treacle and flour were applied to his burns before he was taken another thirty-two kilometres by horse and cart to Stratford. Frederick's burns were too severe, and he died several days later aged fifty-three.

The eldest daughter was fourteen and her twelve-year-old brother Bill worked the farm before and after their father's funeral while Annie looked after their mother. Sarah never recovered from the tragedy. As Annie and Ethel grew up, they took turns staying at home to look after their mother and help Bill on the farm.

Five hundred pounds was paid by Public Works to the family in compensation for the accident. The three children were to inherit one hundred pounds each when they turned twenty-one but most of that money went to nurse and support their mother who died in 1923.

Not long after Bill inherited the farm, the house burnt down. He sold the property and later purchased another in the district.

Annie and Ethel both married, had children and remained living in the region.

Milking Shed 1902. Unknown
Puke Ariki PHO2002–790

Supplejack

The old man had a piece of supplejack that he hung behind the kitchen door. Christ, that hurt. Talking back to Mum, neglecting your chores and coming home drunk from a party when I was at high school, all were reasons to get a few belts across the backside. Thought he was a nasty brutal bastard until much later when I was told about PTSD and wondered whether he just wanted us to stay alive in the theatre of some battle rumbling around inside his head.

* * *

After The Funeral

A dozen people turned up at the house one afternoon. Us kids didn't know who they were and weren't introduced because Dad sent us down to the hayshed below the house. It was weird, them all turning up in their good clothes and my older brother and three younger siblings kicked out of the house. Eventually, we saw a torch beam and thought Dad was coming, but it wasn't him. Two men appeared at the shed door and said that my middle, George was to go with one of them and I was to go with the other. I told them I wasn't going anywhere. My older brother asked where Dad was.

They looked uncomfortable and said it was our father who told them to come and get us. They said Dad couldn't look after five children after our mother had died. No one had even told us she had. All we knew was that Mum had gone to the hospital a week ago.

Family and Dad's friends only wanted children who were old enough to work. The younger ones were just an extra mouth to feed that they couldn't afford.

Dad kept his eldest boy. The other four children were adopted or sent to children's homes. We lost touch with each other until just recently.

I'm eighty-three years old now and met my youngest sister and brother a few weeks ago, sadly the others have passed.

* * *

Sheep Dip

I'm gay. My parents are modern, cool and love me, but my grandfather believed to his dying day that I had fallen into the sheep dip or that I had been exposed to some chemical like Tordon or DDT and they had 'buggered around' with my hormones. Another reason was that I'd drunk molasses from the trough and ingested some saliva from a gestating cow and that had mucked me up. He was a very devout Catholic and believed amongst other things that reading the Bible by candlelight gave him an even deeper understanding of its teachings as it took him back to the period it was written. That righteous belief meant no one had a chance of changing his mind on anything.

* * *

Disprin Didn't Work

Dad was happy to have me back from boarding school for the holidays. He had plenty of jobs on the farm to keep me busy.

The first morning back, I went feeding out with Dad. Going up one step hill track Dad changed gears. The jolt knocked me off the stack of haybales on the tray. As I fell off, my right leg hooked on a length of bailing twine which broke my fall and also my leg. I found myself hanging off the tray, my leg still tied to the bailing twine while I bounced along behind the tractor.

My screaming eventually caught Dad's ear who stopped the tractor at the top of the track. The tray rolled back over me as he fumbled to lock the brake.

Our neighbour heard my screams. He climbed over the boundary fence to see what all the racket was. He and Dad had to carry me back to the fence, lift me over and place me on the empty tray of the neighbour's Land Rover. No helicopter rescue in those days. Back at home I was given a disprin and waited for the ambulance. My tibia was sticking out through my skin. The disprin didn't work.

* * *

A Personal Note

Of course, most fathers today instil in their sons the same values they were taught by their fathers, who in turn learnt them from theirs. The repeated lesson back then, and possibly one of the most important was accepting and dealing with failure because life is filled with it, right? They generally came as boys began to test boundaries as they transitioned from shorts to trousers, chose the style of their haircut, when they were allowed to stay up later and offered a beer, not a shandy, when their voices broke and probably when they were woken at night by a 'wet dream'. Sarcasm and put-downs checked overconfidence or bullied a better performance when the father judged it could be. Those 'rituals' marked when a boy stopped being a child and became an adult. It is worth considering the rituals in place today that help adolescent boys deal with this transition without a father or male role model.

Communities seemed stronger in the decades when these men grew up, when families and neighbours looked out for one another and circled the wagons when support was required. Children were instilled with qualities and values that rewarded their family and community and built their self-esteem because they were judged by them. It was a time when the value of money was learnt by working for it but it was not the sole purpose of life. They looked up to their elders having been taught that their hard work had made their lives a little easier. They knew what sacrifice was and love was a gesture more valued than a word. For some, they were content to stay on the farm or in the town where they were brought up, for others, adulthood gave them an opportunity to move away and establish a new life somewhere else.

The social structure was tight and expectant, holding people to its values. This kept the focus on family. For a son, a simple gesture like a bottle of lemonade, a visit to the picture theatre or a handkerchief tied around a blooded toe was acknowledgement enough he was loved. It was that simple.

In this modern world filled with excuses and blame, individual responsibility seems marginalised. History is filled with fathers and mothers who had plenty of reasons to ignore their responsibilities and take to the hills, but most didn't and yes, some suffered and many still do for their children. The point is they knew the most important responsibility they had was to the child or children they brought into this world.

Listening to the men talk about their fathers made me reflect on the relationship I had with mine. I realised how lucky I was to have had a father growing up. I catch echoes of him sometimes in what I say and do and that is okay now. I accept they are too ingrained to change and will probably reverberate down through the following generations.

* * *

Notes

1. https://online.maryville.edu/blog/cultural-influences-on-childdevelopment/
2. Iron John: A Book About Men (1990) Robert Elwood Bly was an American poet, essayist, activist and leader of the mythopoetic men's movement. The 'Absence of the Father' is a recurrent theme in Bly's work and according to him, many of the phenomena of depression, juvenile delinquency, and lack of leadership in business and politics are linked to it.
3. https://familyfirst.org.nz/2022/10/31/new-report-measures-fatherabsence-in-nz/ Children's Commissioner Laurie O'Reilly described fatherless families as the 'greatest social challenge facing New Zealanders' this was back in 1998.
4. Mitchell, Lindsay, author. https://www.scoop.co.nz/stories/AK2210/S00637/new-reportmeasures-father-
5. Published by Statista Research Department, Jan 18, 2023 https://www.statista.com/statistics/477466/number-of-serious-violentcrimes-by-youth-in-the-us/
6. https://www.chapter2.org.uk/background
7. Jennifer E. Lansford, PhD. https://www.psychologytoday.com/nz/blog/parenting-andculture/202106/the-importance-fathers-child-development
8. https://www.who.int/news-room/fact-sheets/detail/adolescent-mentalhealth
9. Fergueson DM, Horwood LJ (2001) 'The Christchurch health and development Study: Review of findings on Child and Adolescent mental health,' Augst NZJ Psychiatry, 35:287–96]

The Wall Street Crash of October 1929 triggered the Great Depression.

10. A 45% decrease in exports by 1933 and 12% unemployment saw riots in Wellington, Christchurch and Auckland in 1932.
11. Fromm, Erich. The Art of Loving (1957)
12. Ackroyd Peter. The History of England Volume 1. Foundation.
13. *http://www.britannica.com/event/Irish-Civil-War*
14. Okaro is an area in Taranaki, New Zealand.
15. *https://www.irishtimes.com/culture/heritage/why-don't-we-rememberthe-weaver-street-massacre-in-belfast-1.4797959.*

    Girls suffered the most in the bombing. Ellen Johnstone aged eleven, Elizabeth O'Hanlon (12), Rose-Anne McNeill (13), Catherine Kennedy (15) all were killed.

    Maggie Smith (53) and Mary Owen (40) were also murdered.
16. *https://en.wikipedia.org/wiki/New_Zealand_wool_boom*
17. Virginia Woolf, Moments of Being: A Collection of Autobiographical Writing
18. The town became part of the Kingdom of Westphalia in 1807, the First French Empire in 1810, the Kingdom of Hanover in 1814, and the Prussian Province of Hanover in 1866.
19. Weka is a bird that no longer lives in Taranaki, New Zealand.
20. On 10 July 1967, New Zealand decimalised its currency. The pound was replaced by the dollar, which meant its value was almost halved.
21. *https://plato.stanford.edu/entries/nietzsche/*
22. Scientific Name: Collospermum hastatum. Māori name: Kahakaha
23. Tainui *https://waikatotainui.com/* Tainui is the name of one of the great ocean-going canoes in which Polynesians migrated to New Zealand. Chef Hoturoa was the Rangatira of the voyage.
24. *https://teara.govt.nz/en/cartoon/34529/the-wool-boom-1950*
25. New Zealand Lands and Survey had been known as the Crown Lands Department and General Survey Office. On 1 April 1987, the New Zealand Department of Lands and Survey was dissolved and became various other departments, including the New Zealand Department of Survey and Land Information.
26. Stower's book, titled Bloody Gallipoli: has the most accurate casualty figures for Gallipoli. Fifty-three per cent of the thirteen thousand nine

hundred and seventy-seven New Zealand soldiers in that campaign were killed or injured.

27. Penghu, an area in Eastern Taranaki
28. Morori are Polynesian immigrants, indigenous to what is now known as the Chatham Islands. It is suggested they arrived there in the sixteenth century from mainland New Zealand. Their culture developed its own distinctive language, mythology, and art from Māori. It is suggested they came to New Zealand around 1500 CE.
29. Roger Douglas was a member of the Labour Party from 1969–1990. He became the Minister of Finance; floated the New Zealand dollar, introduced corporate practices to state services, sold off state assets, and removed subsidies. The economic policies he introduced were necessary and had a significant impact on farms and rural communities.
30. Today this area encompasses 78,000 hectares of reserve land. It is west of Lake Taupo and is known as the Timber Trail.
31. Moki Mill, Eastern Taranaki ran from 1927–1947.
32. Tainui is the name of one of the great ocean-going canoes in which Polynesians migrated to New Zealand. Chef Hoturoa was the Rangatira of the voyage.
33. James Wattie came from Hawkes Bay where fruit lay rotting on the ground. In 1934, he learnt New Zealand was making Jam with imported Australian fruit. Wattie had no experience in processing fruit but was committed to helping New Zealand fruit growers. During the Depression, he was brave enough to set up a processing plant to make jam. Following that, he began freezing 75 products ranging across meat, poultry, and vegetables. By the beginning of the 1960s, Wattie Canneries Ltd had sales valued at $10 million.
34. The first shipment of refrigerated meat from Port Chalmers, Dunedin to London was in 1882. That was a significant moment for the New Zealand Sheep and later beef industries.
35. Gustavus Ferinand von Tomsky.
36. Taranaki Men Talk by Alison Robinson published by Thurstone Press
37. Private Colin Burn, 18th Battalion, in M. Hutching (ed.) 'A unique sort of battle': New Zealanders remember Crete, 2001, p. 199
38. Thomas Borthwick and Son's first purchased in Wairata in 1902. Thomas (1835–1912) was an apprentice butcher for his grandfather in

Edinburgh. Later he worked as an agent for the New Zealand Loan and Mercantile Company importing meat from New Zealand, in 1882. In 1883, he moved his business to the Smithfield market, foreseeing the potential growth of the frozen meat industry he purchased the Wairata freezing works in 1902.

39. This story blends several versions of what happened to Morrison. The essence is true: the bank was after him; he did set fire to the buildings and kill his livestock; he did go up the hill and shoot himself and was found by a pig hunter's dog several years later.

Bibliography

BOOKS

Ackroyd Peter (2011) The History of England, Volume 1. Foundation Macmillan.
Bly, Robert Elwood (1990) Iron John: A Book About Men.
Church, Ian (1957) The Stratford Inheritance a History of Stratford and Fromm, Erich (2006) The Art of Loving, Harper Perennial Modern Classics (2006).
Greenhill, Stuart (2020) Dante Fog, Austin & McCauley.
Robinson Alison (2004) Taranaki Men Talk, Thurstone Press.
Stowers Richard (2005) Bloody Gallipoli.
Wallace, Neal (2014) When the Farm Gate Opened: The Impact of Rogernomics On Rural New Zealand.
Walter, David (2005) Stratford: Shakespearean Town Under the Mountain, Dunmore Publishing, Wellington, New Zealand.
Whangamomona (1990) Moana Counties, The Heritage Press.

Websites

A History of Apprenticeship In New Zealand by Nicky Murray.
https://core.ac.uk/download/pdf/35461841.pdf

A History of Rannoch. The Menzies.
https://electricscotland.com/history/rannoch8.htm

Centre for social Justice and Department for Work and Pensions.
https://www.chapter2.org.uk/background

Cultural Influences on Child Development.
https://online.maryville.edu/blog/cultural-influences-on-child-development/

Ditta M. Oliker Ph.D. *https://www.psychologytoday.com/us/blog/the-long-reach-childhood/201106/the-importance-fathers*

Family First. *https://familyfirst.org.nz/2022/10/31/new-report-measures-father-absence-in-nz/*

Irish Civil War. *https://www.britannica.com/event/Irish-Civil-War*

Land & Survey. *https://natlib.govt.nz/records/22353251*

Lindsay Mitchell. October 2022

Moore, Cormac. Dr. *https://www.irishtimes.com/culture/heritage/why-don-t-we-remember-the-weaver-street-massacre-in-belfast-1.4797959.*

Moriori. *https://en.wikipedia.org/wiki/Moriori*

New Zealand Wool Boom. *https://en.wikipedia.org/wiki/New_Zealand_wool_boom*

Roger Douglas. *https://en.wikipedia.org/wiki/Roger_Douglas*

Statista Research Department, Jan 18, 2023 *https://www.statista.com/statistics/477466/number-of-serious-violent-crimes-by-youth-in-the-us/*

Tainui. *https://waikatotainui.com/*

Timber Trail. Journey by Discovery. *https://www.timbertrail.nz/history-of-the-trail/*

Wattie, James. CBE. *https://teara.govt.nz/en/1966/wattie-james-cbe*

Weka. *https://www.doc.govt.nz/nature/native-animals/birds/birds-a-z/weka/*

Acknowledgements

Photographers:

Bellringer, Mark: Artist and photographer, lives at THE BANK in Eltham, New Zealand.
Patience, Simeon: Studio, Fashion, Product, and Car photography specialist with an exquisite portraitist's eyes
Piatek: Joanna: runs 'Captured By Friday Photography' based in Kāpiti, New Zealand. She is an accredited and award-winning photographer focusing on "keeping it real" and fun.
Squire, Jenny: Australian photographer, retired. Lives in Gunnedah.

Artist:

Stallard, Jo: Co-founder of Fenton Street Arts Collective; portrait painter, author.
TO ALL THE MEN, their partners and families who found time to talk to me.
Mrs Lash, who provided the information about Frederek Myers.
David Hancock: Photographer, entrepreneur. Lives at THE POST-OFFICE, Eltham.
Richard Pratt: Co-Owner of the Whangamomona Pub and another history buff.

About the Author

Stuart writes in the same fashion as he distils Gin and Whisky at Fenton Arts Collective & Distillery in Stratford, New Zealand. Flavours are distilled to draw out stories that make one ponder, laugh, wept, imagine and reflect on what it is to be human.

This book was inspired by Stuart's novel *Dante Fog* where the central character must return to his childhood to discover the secrets of his father's past life.

Echoes From the Land

Echoes…is a colourful collection of stories from a colourful collection of twenty men. It focuses on the influence their fathers had on them as they grew up. It is a fascinating collection of photographs, poetry, paintings, stories and transcripts supporting a social commentary about the qualities and values of our past.